CLEVELAND TV Tales

VOLUME 2

CLEVELAND TV Tales
VOLUME 2

More Stories from the Golden Age
of Local Television

Mike & Janice Olszewski

GRAY & COMPANY, PUBLISHERS
CLEVELAND

Gray & Company, Publishers
www.grayco.com

ISBN: 978-1-938441-75-2
Printed in the U.S.A.

1

This book is dedicated to our grandparents. We knew some better than others, but all had a profound impact on our lives. On Jan's side, there are John and Anna Blasher, and Andy and Ella Kopkas. From Mike's side it's Anton and Ann Kutis and Frank and Alma Olszewski.

Contents

Preface

Wow! WHEN WE RELEASED *Cleveland TV Tales*, we had no idea we'd get the overwhelming positive response that came our way. We did get some criticism, though, and it was the same from everyone: "We wanted more!"

And you now have it, here in your hands. Once again we're going behind the screen for another look at the remarkable people and events that gave us so many wonderful memories over the years.

When we're out talking about local TV history, a number of folks come out to share their own stories and anecdotes. They ask questions, too—often including this one: "What compelled you to write this book?"

Here's the answer: We didn't want the contributions of Linn Sheldon, Dorothy Fuldheim, Ron Penfound, Ernie Anderson, Betty Cope, Tom Fields, and so many others to be forgotten. Media is like tap water or a lamp. You turn it on when you need it, off when you're done, and you usually don't give it a second thought. The difference is the *people* who make the product you watch on TV. They've stayed with us over the years and even influenced the way we raised our own families.

Audiences today have a lot more options, including cell phones and computers and streaming media and social media . . . What we watch and how we watch is constantly changing. It's unlikely that TV personalities today will have anywhere near the longevity of the people who came before them.

We also needed to clear up some urban legends. For example, no local kids' show host ever flipped out over the air, and Ghoulardi never blew up a live frog on his show. Both of those rumors got legs over the years, but come on. For most of that time, two news-papers—the *Cleveland Press* and *The Plain Dealer*—were in a con-stant battle to scoop each other. Stories like that would have been front-page news—including the firing of the hosts. So many people have come up to us with these wild stories saying, "I saw it with my own two eyes!" Well, we believe that *you* believe you saw it. But it just didn't happen. Let's see the hard evidence, and hearsay isn't hard evidence. The wildest story was that Dorothy Fuldheim purchased WEWS so she could fire Ernie Anderson. Couple of things: She could probably afford to, but Dorothy did not own any part of WEWS. Plus, "Ghoulardi" was on WJW, and Dorothy and Ernie were actually very close friends. When we asked the guy who related the story what he did for a living he said he owned a head shop. As comics great Stan Lee would say, "'Nuff said!"

We were also thrilled (and frankly, relieved) at the number of TV veterans who gave us a thumbs-up for our efforts on the first volume and said, "Keep it coming." Happy to oblige.

So let's warm up our memories of the old family TV set, step through the screen, and see what was going on behind the scenes with some of our favorite personalities. Here are more of the funny, more of the strange, more of the poignant and sometimes down-right weird Cleveland TV Tales!

—*Mike & Janice Olszewski*

Ernie's Legacy

Following in the Footsteps of "Ghoulardi"

THERE'S NO QUESTION THAT Ernie Anderson was one of the biggest stars, if not the biggest, ever to come out of Cleveland television. He was only Ghoulardi for a few years, but that was all the time he needed in order to cast a long shadow over everyone who followed. There were imitators, even some direct rip-offs, but they never held a candle to Ghoulardi.

Every city had them. Vampira in Los Angeles, Zacherle in New York, and on and on. Some, like Elvira, would go national (though in her case, let's face it—it wasn't because she was all that funny). And here's a case of art imitating life. Remember Count Floyd on *SCTV*? Joe Flaherty played the very serious news anchorman Floyd Robertson who had to do double duty on weekends as horror host Count Floyd. He would paint on a widow's peak, put on a Dracula cape and howl like a wolf between comments about the movie. Flaherty based Count Floyd on "Chilly Billy" Cardille, the weatherman at his hometown station in Pittsburgh.

Dick Van Hoene started his "Cool Ghoul" character on radio in 1961. It was a huge hit, and in 1969, he took the character to the new WXIX-TV. Since it was a startup station, Van Hoene was also a fill-in news anchor.

After Ernie Anderson headed west, Cleveland was left without a horror host for a while. Sure, there was Superhost, who did show some monster films, but he was always about comedy.

In 1971, Ernie's former intern, Ron Sweed, convinced WKBF to give him a shot. He put on Ernie's old fright wig, and copied his uniform down to the lab coat, beard and sunglasses with a missing lens. Channel 61 introduced The Ghoul.

"Big Chuck" Schodowski would later say he was surprised Sweed copied Ernie so closely. Sweed would argue that Ernie just sat on the set and he, Sweed, moved around, but there was a bigger difference. Ghoulardi was cerebral, the "thinking man's" horror host. His humor was satire. The Ghoul was slapstick. But for folks too young to remember Ghoulardi, that would do. Sweed actually did pretty well for a while, and his show was picked up at other Kaiser Broadcasting stations. Detroit had never had Ghoulardi, so the audience there believed Sweed had originated the character. Kaiser Broadcasting faded away, and the Ghoul's syndication disappeared as well. Years later, Sweed would still be mistaken for Ghoulardi.

When Channel 61 became WCLQ in 1981, Sweed got another shot. The Froggy character was first seen on Andy Devine's *Andy's Gang* on NBC back in the fifties. His full name was "Froggy, the Gremlin," and he was a gruff-voiced frog puppet in a red jacket who always caused some sort of trouble when he walked on the set. Sweed was old enough to remember Froggy the Gremlin and borrowed the character for his own use. You'll recall the Ghoul show was heavy on fireworks, but what you might not know is that the Channel 61 studios were way up in the woods at Camp Christopher on Ridgewood Road. One night Sweed aired a skit where Froggy, played by Bobby Newhouser, was in a shed that was lit on fire. Think about that. In a forest. Gary Brandt was the general manager, saw the bit, and Sweed was off the schedule.

Columbus had "Fritz the Nite Owl," which debuted on WBNS in 1974. Frederick Peerenboom, a long-time radio/TV personality in Columbus, had cut his teeth doing production for the Army Signal Corps back in the fifties. In fact, that's where he developed a lot of the visual effects he eventually used on the Fritz show. Like other hosts, Fritz would comment on the films, usually over a jazz music bed, and he had plenty of fans in and out of the business. He won five Emmy awards for that role.

A little farther north, "The Baron" held court in Mansfield. Off-screen he was Roger Price, who had hosted some local talk

FRIENDS IN HIGH PLACES: Tim Conway caught up with old friend Ernie Anderson when he came out to Hollywood to film his guest spot on *Gunsmoke*. On the far right is Ken Curtis, who played Festus Haggen. *Cleveland Press Collection, Cleveland State University Archives*

shows, did voice-overs and sold ad time for the station. The Baron's show was on local cable, which allowed for a lot more creativity than the commercial stations. It also took a lot more prep time: ninety minutes just for the makeup! Roger had another character, the "Lone Wino," who did a Foster Brooks–type drunk act with a cowboy hat and a mask.

But there were other players on the show. Roger had been part of an improv troupe that would stop by, and there were taped skits as well. He did the show live every Friday night from 10:00 p.m. to 12:30 a.m. and drew a pretty solid following. Forget the ratings book. The real test was with the sponsor, Shakey's Pizza, which offered a special "Baron" pizza that sold a lot of pies! Roger also made no secret that Ghoulardi was his main inspiration.

It's rare that you see a duo share horror-host duties. You had Bob "Hoolihan" Wells and "Big Chuck" Schodowski (later with "Lil' John" Rinaldi), but the only time they were in costume was in skits. Horror hosts stay in character. Then there were "Frank and Drac."

Shortly after WOIO went on the air, auditions were held for someone to host the Saturday night creature feature. As general manager Dennis Thatcher put it, that form of vaudeville was far from dead. "It seems to be part of an independent station's evolution. First, you get your children's programming in order, then your movies, then a horror-movie host."

Some of the auditions were predictable. Thatcher told *The Plain Dealer*, "Everybody had a good costume, and if they were female, they had a low-cut gown. But nobody had the ability to write." That is, until Allen Christopher and Robert Kokai walked through the door.

It's also unusual that you get someone with their unique experience in local TV, but these two had show biz backgrounds. They were both from Cleveland and had headed west for a shot at the big time in Los Angeles.

Christopher was a voice student and had performed at the Old Stone Church and Blossom Music Center. He was even a Kenley Player for a time. He was bitten by the TV bug when he worked with Bill Baker, who would later go on to New York's WNET. Christopher also had some TV experience in L.A. He had directed some music videos and even pitched some pilot shows, but no dice.

Pretty much the same thing with Kokai. When he graduated from Otterbein College, he worked a couple of seasons with the Great Lakes Shakespeare Festival. Then he heard California calling and headed west. Oddly enough, that's where he met Christopher, and they decided to work as a team. Still, it's a rough business, and there are only so many slots for talented people. After a time their chances in Northeast Ohio looked a lot more promising than waiting tables in Hollywood, so back they came, and with them, valuable experience.

NO PRESSURE THERE! Bob "Hoolihan" Wells, "Lil John" Rinaldi and "Big Chuck" Schodowski all hosted the late night slot left open when Ghoulardi left the Channel 8 airwaves. *Fox8 TV*

Thatcher recalled that they came loaded for bear. Professional right off the bat. They arrived with a twenty-five-page script, and then there were the costumes. Christopher was heavily made up as a Frankenstein character and Kokai was Drac, and he put a lot into the Dracula getup.

Kokai also pretty much wrote most of the material. In a *Plain Dealer* profile piece he said Dracula was an early inspiration. "As a kid I was enthralled by Dracula, right down to the model kits, buttons, and the games. In second grade, a teacher told my parents that if they didn't take the stuff away my mind would be warped." Or, in hindsight, maybe get a job! John Lennon's Aunt Mimi was famous for the quote, "The guitar's all very well, John, but you'll never make a living out of it." Kokai's teacher might have said the same thing about vampire fangs. He said part of Dracula's appeal was that "he was a hopeless romantic . . . and no one told him when to go to bed!"

WOIO gave them a contract, and soon afterward, Frank and Drac hit the airwaves. Some of the skits were pretty innovative and even topical. They took over Elvira's time slot at 11:30 p.m. on Halloween night, October 31, 1987. They did their own version of *The People's Court*, with complaints about Frankenstein breaking into a house and eating the kids. *Action Monster News* had Frank singing the weather, "Tonight it's going to get dark, and then darker . . . and then really dark!" And it could get kind of gory, too, but no one took it seriously. Drac sang a parody of "Peg in My Heart" with a stake in his chest and blood pouring out. Then there were the Vampirettes . . . three scantily clad assistants named Bambi, Thumper, and Boom-Boom, or as *The Plain Dealer* described them: "a feminist's nightmare."

Frank and Drac weren't on the station long, maybe a year, but they did leave a video footprint. Their message was that in the really good horror films, "the people cheer for the monsters."

When it comes to longevity, no one beats Keven Scarpino. He's been the "Son of Ghoul" since 1986, the longest continuous horror show host in the country. No one else even comes close, and he's the first to tell you, "It ain't easy!" He took the name after winning a Ghoulardi lookalike contest at the old Cleveland Agora in 1982, but never really thought about TV until a couple of years later.

Like Frank and Drac, Keven had a show biz background, but his was in music. A guy in Canton was performing under the name "Cool Ghoul," and on the way back from one of his gigs, Keven stopped to watch Three Stooges reruns that the Cool Ghoul was hosting for the Muscular Dystrophy Telethon. The two struck up a conversation, and the Cool Ghoul invited Keven to one of his tapings at WOAC in Canton. That led to him working the camera when a crewman didn't show, and an eventual production job at the station. Later, when the Cool Ghoul quit, Keven won the audition to replace him. It was a thirteen-week tryout, and Keven didn't think his run would last any longer than that. But then there were another thirteen weeks, and thirteen after that, and he's been on the air ever since . . . but to this day, he never looks beyond the next thirteen weeks.

The key to being a successful horror host is original material, and Keven brought a load of new stuff every week. Sometimes it worked, sometimes it didn't, but he wanted to show people he was having fun and they could join in if they liked.

By 1987, he had started getting more attention and lots of offers for personal appearances, when he was sued by Ronald D. Sweed. That's right, "The Ghoul." Keven came to Stark County Common Pleas Court with two attorneys, one representing WOAC-TV and one he had hired. The lawyers were obviously not used to cases like this. As Keven recalls, "After that first court appearance, I didn't think they knew what was going on. I didn't have much hope."

He's also the first to admit he was wrong, big time!

The papers jumped on the story. *The Canton Repository* ran this headline: "Channel 67's 'Son of Ghoul' sued by 'dad'."

Sweed claimed Keven and WOAC/Massillon were "violating his rights, damaging his business, misleading and deceiving the public." The suit pointed to a personal appearance at Dragway 42 in West Salem earlier that year featuring "Son of Ghoul." Sweed claimed Scarpino was copying his Ghoul character and WOAC was airing a show similar to the one he had syndicated in Cleveland and three other cities.

Here's what Sweed wanted: A permanent restraining order and that Keven and his TV station "be enjoined from using 'The Ghoul' character, mannerisms, stage, and props, and the words 'Son of Ghoul' or any imitation as a trade name or slogan." That wasn't all. He also demanded an accounting of "all business conducted by them using the character, stage and props, and name; a judgment for all profits they made from that use" and, oh yes—$500,000 in damages! Sweed was quoted in *The Plain Dealer* saying, "He didn't create anything on his own." The lawyers and Keven disagreed. The *Akron Beacon Journal* called it "a judicial blood test." The paper also quoted Sweed as saying the "Son of Ghoul' is 'diminuating' the

SEND IN THE CLONES! Ron Sweed resurrected Ghoulardi's fright wig, lab coat, and phony beard and moustache when The Ghoul debuted on WKBF, Channel 61. *Author's collection*

rights and profits of The Ghoul." (And who wants to be "diminuated?")

The *Beacon Journal* quoted "Big Chuck" Schodowski as saying Sweed was Ghoulardi's "mail boy" back in the early 1960s. This promised to be a very compelling trial. There was even speculation that it could turn into a jury trial, although *The Repository* suggested that could be difficult, since the only peer of Sweed's Ghoul character was the defendant.

One of Keven's attorneys set up a blackboard in the courtroom. There were several categories listed and the lawyer questioned Sweed about each one. Number one was the name. Sweed said he had laid claim to that. Yet Kaiser Broadcasting actually copyrighted it in 1975. "Do you own the music?" No. They crossed that one out. "Do you own the camera angles? No. That's out, too . . . and the claims fell, one after another. Then there was a dispute over Froggy the Gremlin. Yeah, Keven had used Froggy, but what claim did Sweed have on him? Andy Devine had introduced that character many years before.

Then, the attorney for WOAC, Jacob Hess, took a plastic frog out of a brown paper bag and set it on his shoulder. He asked Sweed, "If I put this frog on my shoulder, am I copying your character?"

Keven's attorney, Allen Krash, who had a reputation for not showing emotion, reportedly laughed hard enough to bring tears to his eyes. The judge got a kick out of it, too. Sweed reportedly stifled a smile but admitted that he had no exclusive rights to any of the words and actions used by Keven. But he claimed there were too many similarities to be mere coincidence.

The attorneys drilled Sweed on how successful he had been at finding work as the Ghoul since January 1985, when the show was taken off the air. Sweed said his main source of income was his job at a General Electric plant where he'd worked since 1979. He then testified that the show had been turned down in San Francisco, L.A., Chicago and other major markets. He also admitted that the Son of Ghoul was not available or marketed to any of those markets.

It made for some great courtroom theater, but the case might well have met its ultimate end in the office of Keven's attorney.

Remember that look-alike contest Keven had won at the Agora? He had a videotape of the event. It was hosted by Sweed, who was in costume, and sure enough, Keven was dressed just like him. They were both wearing lab cats, fright wigs, phony beards and sunglasses with a lens popped out: the same outfit Ernie Anderson had worn as Ghoulardi. Then came the announcement: Keven was named the winner . . . and Sweed declared him "Son of Ghoul!" There's more. Sweed had even showed that tape on his own show.

But Keven's on-screen attire now was a cape, tuxedo tails, and a top hat. He looked like a beatnik funeral director. The attorney had a big smile: "We just won this case!"

The court agreed. Judge Sheila Farmer wrote that both characters were descended from a show business tradition that dated back to Boris Karloff, one of the kings of the Universal Studios monster movies who had later hosted TV's *Thriller*. Farmer said the average viewer wasn't going to confuse these two. She added, for the record, "Horror show hosts can be categorized as being offbeat characters, hosting old movies, performing comic skits and appealing to the preteen to mid-twenties age group."

Keven summed it up this way to the *Utter Trash* website: "He claimed that I was stealing his character, which he had never created. It ended up that he didn't own anything, and the judge found that I was free to do what I wanted to do." Keven continue to do just that for many years afterward. The lawsuit quickly went down in flames, and the Son of Ghoul came out the big winner. It was on to WAOH in Akron, and the Son of Ghoul era continued.

Son of Ghoul had a long list of celebrities appear on his show, including the Monkees, Dee Snyder of Twisted Sister, Robin Trower, and too many others to list here. There was even an exchange with Paul McCartney. But one of his biggest fans was the brilliant guitarist Stevie Ray Vaughan. They hit it off when Keven interviewed him before a show, and had kept in touch, and Stevie made it a point to invite Keven to his gigs. He also asked for Son of Ghoul discs to play on his tour bus, and Keven was happy to comply. In August 1990, after a gig with Eric Clapton, Vaughan was killed in a helicopter crash. He was inducted into the Rock and Roll Hall of Fame in 2015. Not long after his death, Keven got word that Stevie had loved watching his shows as he traveled the country. Those Son of Ghoul DVDs were found in his personal effects when they cleaned out his tour bus.

When you're a horror host, you don't turn down gigs, and you tend to travel a lot. If you've got a good act and you're lucky, you keep getting offers. You also come across a lot of characters. One

HEIR APPARENT: Keven Scarpino was dubbed "Son of Ghoul" at a contest hosted by Ron Sweed. Scarpino would go on to be the longest continually running horror host in the country. *Keven Scarpino*

key to being a successful show host of any kind is when someone shows you they have the stuff, you step back and let the big dog eat. You don't have to be center of attention. You think about the good of the overall show.

Ron Huffman wanted a career in TV, but that didn't seem likely. Dwarfism and a speech impediment limited his options. Then he crossed paths with the Son of Ghoul at a public appearance. Keven took him under his wing, renamed him "Fidge," and put him to work on the set, doing skits and live appearances. Fidge became a fan favorite, and he and Keven clicked when they appeared together. They had sort of an Abbott and Costello relationship, with the Son of Ghoul playing the straight man with a short fuse.

Big Chuck had Lil' John and Keven had Fidge, but there was a huge difference between the two. John Rinaldi was a regular guy who was short of stature; Fidge was like Froggy, a gremlin. You never knew what would happen when he entered a room, but for sure something was going to happen, and it would probably be an event. For a time, the Son of Ghoul hosted a live, weekly two-hour quiz show called *House of Fun and Games* with Fidge as his co-host. Fidge was a special guest at pop culture conventions, signed hundreds of autographs, and had his own t-shirts. At one point, he was even featured on the MTV series *True Life*. Sadly, he died way too soon, in his early thirties. But he could say to the end that he had lived his dream. Keven aired a two-hour retrospective honoring him a few days after his death.

Cable access TV is a convenient way to get screen time, and that means a lot for the next generation of horror hosts. There's the "Yummy Mummy," actress Janet Jay, who calls herself Janet Decay, whose costume includes an ankh surrounding her left eye and a bizarre white contact lens.

Her co-host is a gorilla, Grimm Gorri, played by her producer, James Harmon. She trades the mummy bandages for camouflage when she acts as "Jungle Janet," assistant to "Jungle Bob" Tuma. "Jungle Bob" has carried on in the tradition of an earlier Cleveland TV character, "Jungle Larry," for years on television and in personal appearances.

"Jungle Bob" also appeared every week on the Son of Ghoul's show. In one of those appearances, Bob also found himself in serious trouble.

Bob knew the proper way to handle animals but, as both he and his predecessor Jungle Larry could tell you, animals are still wild creatures with minds of their own. Sometimes they don't take cues very well. As a weekly feature on the Son of Ghoul show, Jungle Bob brought a wide range of critters. A lot of the humor came from Keven's fear of what was in the box: scorpions, tarantulas, hissing cockroaches . . . and on one particular week, a bull snake.

After introducing Bob, Keven made it a point to stay at arm's length and handed "Jung" the microphone. As long as that snake was out of the box, he did the interview from a distance. Bull snakes can get as big as six feet. This one wasn't that large, but you couldn't miss him, and he had a mind of his own, right from the start. Bob gave some background on the snake, holding the mic in one hand and trying to manage his "guest" with the other. Let's also make clear that the snake was not cooperative, so Bob literally had his hands full. No way Keven would touch it!

"A bull snake has a little bit of an attitude when you first pick him up," Bob said, "and we would find that out soon enough. He seemed to be pretty passive at first, but he was still constantly moving. It's a snake! That's what they do. I've been handling him all day, so he won't bite. He hissed at me a couple of times, but that's about it." He might have wanted to clear that with the snake. As he went on about the way snakes shed their skin and some other fun facts while holding the reptile up for the camera, the snake got excited. Bob handed Keven the mic as the snake slithered up Bob's arm to the back of his neck and . . . YOW! . . . sank his teeth into him! As Keven checked out the wound, Bob hesitantly said, "I'll be okay," but it was obvious the snake had done some damage.

Time to wrap up the segment. Playing to the camera, Bob laughingly gave out his website and pretended to collapse, although Keven looked and sounded really concerned. "Call 911!"

Back to the movie.

Want glamour, fame, and fortune? Horror hosting is not the profession for you. Your TV show is the first rung on the ladder; your website and personal appearances bring in the real money. That means you make it a point to spend whole weekends pressing the flesh at the big shows. At huge conventions like Steve Haynes' Cinevent, Mike Savene's MonsterFestMania, and others, you spend a lot of time on the show floor. Long hours, and even longer for Keven because the Son of Ghoul will often host Saturday morning cartoons and play with his band late into the night. Sleep is a luxury, and you get it when you can.

Pop culture has awards for every genre. The Rondos are handed out to folks who have shown outstanding effort in promoting classic horror films and TV. They're named after Rondo Hatton, a little known B-movie villain who was so remarkably ugly he could scare a bulldog off a baloney wagon. The trophy is an exact replica of his face. Yet this is a major award for the industry. The biggest and most influential names have taken home Rondos. Filmmakers George Romero and Ray Harryhausen, TV hosts Vampira and Zacherle, Ray Bradbury . . . you get the idea. They're handed out at the annual Wonder Fest Convention in Kentucky, and when Ghoulardi got the nod, the Son of Ghoul was asked to accept on his behalf.

The Forrest Ackerman Award (or "Forrie") also carries a lot of weight. It's named after the editor of *Famous Monsters of Filmland* magazine, who revived the careers of many actors from the old Universal Studio monster films. It's awarded at Ron Adams' "Monster Bash," and is one of the highlights of the convention weekend. A huge crowd shows up for this event, and many had come just to see the awards ceremony.

Keven Scarpino hits the ground running every year at Monster Bash and keeps moving until the show ends for the weekend—showing cartoons in the morning, Three Stooges shorts at noon, and then working his merchandise table in between. The night before the ceremony, he also did a special concert with horror-film legend Arch Hall, Jr. (also a very talented and accomplished rock guitarist). On Saturday night, the Bash projects classic movies on the side of the hotel. It's like a drive-in, and afterward, everyone heads inside for the awards ceremony. Almost everyone.

Keven was tired, dog tired, but he knew better than to put his head on a pillow. They wouldn't be able to pry him out of the bed. After a long day, he was hauling equipment out to his van and had to sit down. Next thing you know, he was sawing wood. Snoring away! Meanwhile, Ron Adams was announcing that year's Forrie went to . . . the Son of Ghoul! Applause! Ron waited a moment, looked around, and said . . . "The Son of Ghoul." Nothing. "Son of Ghoul. Keven?" He had no clue he was the recipient of that year's award until the next morning.

Yes, being a horror host isn't easy!

"They tortured me at Channel 5 . . ."

Mark Koontz

MARK KOONTZ TOOK HIS career seriously. Some thought too seriously, and that's why he seemed an easy target—and not just at one station. The ultimate trick on Koontz was played at WEWS and detailed in *Cleveland TV Tales*, but there were plenty more pranks after that.

One classic was set up after Channel 5 producer Bob Woods found a blank sheet of American Meteorological Society letterhead. It might have been stuck on the back of a letter, but there it was, and it looked very official. This was too valuable to use for scrap paper.

You might remember Woods from the "Eyewitness Newsreel," which ran every night. He created that feature and voiced it, too. Now he and Don Mertens were about to create a little mayhem. He showed Don the paper and said, "We can't let this go." They wrote a letter to Koontz complimenting him on his accomplishments. Don remembers it read something like: "As you know, the American Meteorological Society meets once a year. This time our annual meeting will be held in Boston, and we would be very grateful if you would consider being our keynote speaker." It suggested he go ahead and book airfare and a room, and the AMS would square up with him on all expenses. They left the letter on Koontz' desk.

Pretty much the whole newsroom was in on the joke, but they shared his excitement. Buttons are bursting off Koontz's chest! He even asked general manager Ed Cervenak if he could mention it on the air, but that wasn't going to happen. Even so. Koontz! Keynote!

A few days before, Woods pulled Mertens aside and said, "We'd better do something. He might be booking flights and a room that's not refundable!" This was going to be awkward, but they finally let him in on the joke.

TV is transitional. Everyone will tell you that you go in day by day wondering if you have a job. Everyone. Koontz eventually got canned at WEWS, but he wasn't done with Cleveland TV yet.

Just a short time later, in March 1981, he started at Channel 8 as the noon and weekend weatherman. He'd work Saturday and Sunday and three times during the week. Plus, he'd fill in for Dick Goddard, which was a high-profile gig! His addition to the staff was seen as a positive, though *The Plain Dealer*'s James Ewinger gave him a back-handed compliment that October: "Mark Koontz seems finally to have passed the throes of puberty." Still, life was looking pretty good . . . but people liked to pull tricks at Channel 8, too.

Don Mertens was the brains behind many of those jokes at Channel 5, and when Koontz landed a gig at Channel 8, Don took a call from that station asking for a list of pranks that had already been pulled on him. The word was, Channel 8 repeated some of them with the same results!

Koontz wasn't the only target. A producer at Channel 8 used to get his share, usually from Dale Solly. Many of the folks at home think TV newsrooms are like the movie *The Front Page* or *All the President's Men*. Hard-nosed journalists who fight for scoops, and when they're not doing that, they're pounding a typewriter at a hundred miles an hour. That's not usually the case.

Dale could get really creative. Okay, maybe some of the stuff was a little sophomoric, but it was still funny. Solly would rub Limburger inside the drawers of the producer's desk or fill his boots with water and let them turn to blocks of ice in the parking lot. Once he nailed a guy's shoes to the floor. You know, the usual stuff. Bowling in the hallways, which accounted for the huge dent in the wall.

Sometimes the damage was a little more extensive. One day

MARKED MAN: Mark Koontz was a popular target for practical jokes . . . and not because of his hair!
Cleveland Press Collection, Cleveland State University Archives

Dale was playing Frisbee with Tana Carli when the disc flew into the original "On Air" sign that had been around since day one. You guessed it. Shattered glass everywhere. Dale just swept it up and hoped no one would miss it.

Now, back to Koontz.

Ad-libbing is dangerous. Sometimes things are said on the air that you wish you could take back. Isabel Tener would do cooking demonstrations, and in the warmer months would cook outside. Rick DeChant was producing the noon broadcast on a really nice day and suggested they do grilling tips in the sunshine. And why not have Koontz do his weather out there, too? Koontz was a pretty affable guy on the air. He interacted well with the guests and no one had second thoughts about him working with Isabel. The weather played into grilling so they could go back and forth as needed. On the menu that day were flank steaks, and sometimes you have to tenderize them. Isabel had a high voice reminiscent of Dan Ackroyd impersonating Julia Child ("Save the liver!"). Anyway, Isabel mentioned you could tenderize meat easily with a little metal hammer to soften it up. That doesn't necessarily make for compelling TV, so Isabel asked Koontz to give her a hand with the hammer while she worked on the vegetables. Koontz held the hammer in one hand, the steaks, in the other and said, "I'll stand here and beat my meat." That's funnier than "Save the liver!"

Again, let's stress that moments like that happen to everyone. You just hope that no one hears it, or no one believes it when you pass it on.

Dave Buckel was anchoring with Susan Howard; Vince Cellini was on sports. They would toss to each other with little conversational bits, a natural transition. This was the day that Dick Russ' wife, Chris, gave birth to their son, Peter. The anchors congratulated the couple for the new addition and handed it to Cellini, who said he was also "happy for Dick's little Peter." Let's move on.

It's not that anyone disliked Mark Koontz. He was just so focused, and that struck people as funny. Koontz wanted every broadcast to be his best, which is commendable, and sometimes he took issue with criticism. Rick DeChant recalls an incident when Koontz filled in for Dick Goddard. He came back in to the newsroom and someone wanted to speak with him on the phone. Koontz picked up he receiver, there were some, "Yeah. Uh-huhs." and out of nowhere, Koontz yelled, "Well, what the **** do you know about television, Mom!?" The handset slammed down, and so did a coffee cup, which smashed into pieces. Goddard's desk was next to Casey Coleman's, and a chunk of the cup flew into Casey's typewriter. With a deadpan look and without missing a beat, Casey took the piece out of the typewriter and said, "Mark, I take it Mom didn't like the show."

Rick DeChant is a very funny guy, a great standup comic. You'll remember him as the "Samurai Weatherman" on the *Big Chuck and Lil' John* show. He could also come up with a good prank at the snap of a finger.

There used to be a place on East 9th Street across from the Roxy Theater called Jean's Fun House. They sold trinkets and practical jokes. Rick stopped in to get cigarette loads, the slivers that would explode when you lit your smoke. Mark Koontz smoked at that point. Do we have to tell you what happened next?

Koontz had a brand new deck of cigarettes on his desk. It was already opened, and Rick got someone to divert his attention while he loaded the cigarette. He even pulled it out just slightly so Koontz would take that one out first. Well, he did and everyone but him was in on the joke. They thought he would light up in the newsroom. That wasn't happening. It was just a few minutes to air for the noon show. When's he going to pull out the lighter? Koontz made a stop in the rest room, and about eight people ran to stand outside the door. A few even followed him into the john. There should be a pretty good echo . . . the bang, and then the reaction. Still didn't happen.

Dick Russ was an eyewitness. "There was much more which led up to that incident," he says. "At least ten or fifteen minutes went by until Koontz lit up the smoke; maybe twenty or twenty-five. A steady stream of guys would come in and out of the restroom, where Koontz and I were applying our makeup. He was to the left of me at the sinks with his back to the urinals. Guys who had just taken a leak two minutes before came back in and kind of pretended, glancing over their shoulder, hoping to witness the big moment.

"People are started counting the seconds. Is he going to light that smoke or what? It was hilarious, and after about ten minutes, we started to worry the long line of guys coming into the restroom might tip Koontz off that something was up. I did my best to stretch my makeup session from its usual five to seven minutes to around fifteen or twenty. This was all in the 11:30 a.m. to noon time lead-up to the noon news we did together for so many years."

Koontz finally did light up in the hallway and . . . POW! He wasn't happy, especially when a part of the paper or maybe a shred of tobacco went into his eye. Rick came clean and apologized and, fortunately, Koontz didn't react nearly as badly as he could have.

It became that evident that Dick Goddard wasn't going anywhere, and Koontz decided to look for a position that would use him more. Channel 8 tried to persuade him not to go, but his mind was made up. One of the last things he said to some folks at Channel 8 was, "They tortured me at Channel 5 for seven years . . . and you people are no better!"

We mentioned earlier that practical jokes went on all the time and anyone could be on the receiving end, even management. Earl Keyes was one of the old-timers at WEWS. He played Mr. Nicholsworth on Captain Penny's show, and directed a lot of the live stuff there, including Mr. Jingeling. As it turns out, he eventually got to play him for many years, and his earliest shows were at WEWS. Mr. Jingeling had a huge throne on set, very regal and very heavy. Hundreds of pounds, and . . . again, Don Mertens came up with an idea. Garry Ritchie was news director at that time, but he didn't have a really big office. He would lock the door behind him when he left for the night. Don got together with some folks from the crew and took a forklift to put the throne in Garry's office! This thing weighed a ton. They got it through a false ceiling and maneuvered it so Garry had a hell of a time getting into his office. It took some great minds most of the day to figure out how to get it back on the set because it didn't fit through the door.

News anchors got their share, too. Ted Henry did a week-long series on car theft for the eleven o'clock news. Vida Gaizutis was the editor and producer for the series, and it showed how not to be a victim. Vida helped sneak Ted's keys, and that night after the last segment aired, Ted went out to find his car missing. After a few nervous minutes, he was told it was in another lot.

Cars were sometimes at risk at WEWS. In those days, cars were at risk anywhere downtown, but one day someone came in to say someone was trying to break in to Liz Richards' car. Jack Starr, who worked as a photographer at Channel 5, was also a full-time cop. He ran out to the lot, but Liz got there first and, as Don recalls, she was "pounding the hell out of the guy." He probably felt relieved when Starr took him away, and should have. Liz was known to carry a handgun in her purse!

Don took his lumps, too. They were a lot more creative. How the chief editor for the six o'clock news was able to swing two weeks off is anyone's guess, but Don took his vacation and came back to a surprise. Don walked in at 2:30 p.m. and Bob Woods came up to him and said, "We have a major problem!" The seven film editors who worked on the six o'clock show had all picked up and quit! "But we do have some new people. We need you to train them." "Train them?" Mertens responded. "We have a show to get out now!" One "new girl" held up two pieces of film and said they were "sticky." After about a half an hour of this, the original crew returned and told Don the rookies were drama students from Cleveland State. The crew put together the show, and after a time Don's hair grew back, too.

The Morning Exchange

IT'S HARD TO ARGUE with success, and after twenty-seven years on the air, no one could deny that *The Morning Exchange* was successful. But there were plenty of twists and turns along the way.

The show was created in 1972 by the station's general manager, Don Perris, and executive producer Bill Baker. There was some risk involved. Who's going to take the time to watch morning talk? You get the kids off to school, maybe you have some at home . . . who's got the time? Sure, shows like *Romper Room* were on the air in the morning and had been around for years, and with most women still at home—not in the workforce—there was an available audience. But no one knew whether this format was going to work unless they tried it. So they did.

Carol Story, the founding associate producer for the new show, said there was a lot of secrecy before *The Morning Exchange* went on the air. She remembers being told, "Don't tell anyone what we're doing."

The Morning Exchange with Alan Douglas debuted on January 3, 1972. The "Exchange" in the name referred to the exchange of ideas. The show's first guests were Miss America Phyllis George and Cleveland Mayor Ralph Perk. In a pretty big step, for the first time ever viewers could watch *and* call in and talk to world leaders, authors, celebrities, and local experts. Contests, classified ads, the Shopper's Exchange, live phone calls from viewers, "Backtalk"—all were intended to give viewers a voice in the broadcast. As Carol remembers it, "People didn't call in to TV shows, but now they had an opportunity to talk to a famous author, Burt Reynolds, a doctor . . . anyone!"

Sometimes the hosts would open the phones to fill in for a guest who didn't show. A producer would screen calls in the engineer's booth, and the next stop was straight on the air. But the real significance of the show was that it reflected current events not only in Northeast Ohio, but nationwide. Carol says the guest list was a reflection of early 1970s America. "We had feminists like Gloria Steinem and Bella Abzug, and even folks like Jimmy Hoffa, who was president of the Teamsters Union."

Dorothy Fuldheim gave *The Morning Exchange* a boost because every prominent name who came through Cleveland wanted to be interviewed by "Big Red," and now the *Morning Exchange* set was just down the hall.

The WEWS "Video Vault" web page shows a clip from the early days of the show and includes this quote from videographer Bob Seeley describing the show: "Bill Baker, who was the executive producer of *The Morning Exchange*, decided that the first hour would be mostly news and information—almost like the morning news shows now—and the second hour would be long-form."

Alan Douglas, who had been around for years on radio and the old WKBF, channel 61, sat behind a desk on the *Morning Exchange* set. Don Webster was the announcer and co-host, and Joel Rose did the news. A couple of months later, Liz Richards joined the staff, replacing Webster.

How do you sell an untested format? The station offered commercial spots starting at $1 per second, but that price would go up along with the ratings. It didn't take long for the ad rates to escalate.

We discuss Douglas and his career in detail in our first volume of *Cleveland TV Tales*, but the bottom line is, he soon left *The Morning Exchange*. His wife had died, his hearing was going bad and, after a sabbatical, he took a radio gig and didn't come back. Later, he committed suicide.

Douglas was replaced by Fred Griffith.

"Don Webster hosted briefly, but then they asked Fred Griffith, who was public affairs director, to fill in," said Jane Temple (who joined the show two years later). "At the time they didn't think it was permanent. Everyone said, 'He's too mild-mannered.'

There's no question he's intelligent and very erudite. Well-edu-cated. They just felt he was too bland, and ironically, it was that level of even-handedness with everybody that became one of his biggest selling points."

Published reports at the time claimed that the consultant advising the station, Frank Magid Associates, really didn't care for Fred. They summed him up as "too aloof and cold ever to be of significant use to your station."

Ernie Sindelar, the operations manager, disagreed. He found Fred to be "warm and well rounded." News director Garry Ritchie. saw a definite chemistry, and he summed up Fred as "avuncular" and "smart." (Liz he considered naive; Rose was "Peck's bad boy," and when Jan Jones came on board years later, he noticed "vulnerability.")

Temple says she thought the three hosts worked well because they weren't acting; they were just themselves. "What you see has to be what you get. That means you can be a crook, as long as you're honest about being a crook. You just have to be what you are," she explains. "What you see in Fred is a smart and kind man. What you see with Joel Rose is a kind of cantankerous, but witty guy. Kind of a curmudgeon, but that's who he was." And together with Liz, the ingénue, they formed a pretty solid team.

Producers soon scrapped the old set, brought in some couches and comfortable chairs, and made it look like your living room at home. It would pretty much stay with that same format for decades. Everyone worked hard, but they still crossed their fingers with each ratings book.

Bill Baker created a system of calling people he knew who were watching at home to ask whether they found the show or segment interesting. Initially this included his wife and some of her friends; later associate producers would take a weekly "late-day" to stay home and watch the show, calling in on the "hotline" to say whether or not the guests were really working. Soon, there was no need. *The Morning Exchange* was getting close to seventy percent of the audience!

TOP OF THE MORNING: Fred Griffith, Liz Richards and Joel Rose welcomed thousands of guests over the years both in and out of the water. *Cleveland Press Collection, Cleveland State University Archives*

Perris and Baker's plan was paying off in spades! It was a juggernaut, and if you had something you wanted the public to know about, *The Morning Exchange* was your first stop . . . if they could fit you in.

There was no shortage of guests. The locals lined up, but Cleveland also became a must-stop location on every author's tour.

"We would go to the book conventions in L.A. and New York and meet with all the publishers," Terry Moir said. "We would explain what the show was, and one of the original associate producers, Carol Story, established the deepest relationships with them."

The Morning Exchange also had an attractive offer: they would foot the bill for the author's stay at Stouffer's Inn on the Square (in the early days, it was the very elegant Hollenden House and later the trendy and cool Swingos). The station had two rooms permanently reserved in exchange for a 30-second spot plugging the hotel at the end of every show. All they wanted in return was exclusivity when the author was on their dime. No problem there! Authors could do as much radio as they wanted, but *The Morning Exchange* had the TV rights.

Many publishers made Cleveland the first major market stop after New York City. Authors would appear on *The Morning Exchange*, and the publicist would get a report from a producer about how the author did on air. Carol said, "They might hear that the author needs to talk more about this, less about that. Maybe look more at the anchor or dress differently."

It was common for an author to fly into town and sell several hundred copies of the new book just by appearing on *The Morning Exchange*. An author would often get two segments. First was the interview, and the show host might even offer copies of the book to, say, the first five callers. After commercials, the show would take calls for the author.

The Morning Exchange also benefited from a very aggressive Bill Baker, whom Carol describes as having "the balls of a gorilla." If a guest was hesitant about appearing, Baker would be on the phone saying, "Look, you're never going to be successful if you don't do this show!" Most people came around to his way of thinking.

Everyone has an opinion, and Roldo Bartimole became well known locally for offering his as an aggressive journalist with an influential newsletter, *Point of View*. In a June, 1975, issue, Roldo called *The Morning Exchange* the "Morning Sell," and he didn't hold back. He wrote, "If you have ANYTHING but an idea to peddle, take it to 3001 Euclid Avenue any Monday through Friday from 8:00 a.m. to 10:00 a.m. for the *Morning Sell*. That's where they shuffle through, between commercials, hairdressers, cake decorators, faith healers and every author of a fast-sell fad book that brushes his or her teeth in Cleveland."

Roldo described the format as a "stacked deck" and called the way the show approached some topics "premeditated murder." He also didn't like the commercial rates they charged: $110 for a ten-second spot, which Bartimole called "an expensive ride, but the some ninety-thousand viewers (seventy percent women and almost twice the NBC *Today* audience here) are apparently worth the price to advertisers. The cost for ten seconds is nearly triple the original cost for *Morning Exchange* time."

Then he dissected the hosts. "There's Fred Griffith, the nice guy. To dislike smiling Fred is to hate children. But he's trading his smile for personality success." Joel Rose? "A wasted wit, immobilized by a cynicism of acceptance." Bartimole didn't hold back on Liz Richards, who, he said, "willingly plays the dumb female."

However, according to Jane Temple, the prevailing philosophy at all Scripps Howard Broadcasting stations was that viewers were all intelligent and broadcasters should never talk down to them, and that information and education should always be a free service of the broadcast. Jane said one of the goals of *The Morning Exchange* was to offer free information. "You didn't have to get the product. You didn't have to get the book to learn something." Carol Story agrees. She recalls Don Perris stressing to her, "You are not to cave in to the sales department. If it's not good TV, it doesn't get on the TV."

You get a feeling that Roldo just didn't care that much for *The Morning Exchange*.

But a lot of people did, and more were tuning in every week.

"When *The Morning Exchange* went on the air, there was

nothing else," Jane Temple said. "Bear in mind that there were three VHF channels and most women were not working, so you watched one of those channels. Everyone who was anyone who came anywhere near Ohio got on *Morning Exchange*."

Terry Moir echoed that. "I knew at the time it was happening that it was the best job I was ever going to have," she said. "The only limits to the job were the limits of your imagination. We had an outrageous travel budget. I can remember flying in psychic window washers from New Jersey, and a woman who had a potato chip shaped like Jesus. We had to do two hours a day, five days a week. We had cards on a board, color-coded by subject matter. We would grade the guests, and Fred would say, 'If we educated, if we informed, if we entertained, if people want to come back and see us tomorrow, we did our job.'"

Terry and Jane were two of the veterans who helped *The Morning Exchange* evolve over the years. Jane had been in progressive rock radio when WNCR and WMMS were just cutting their teeth. She switched to producing television after a conversation with Dave Patterson at WEWS at a press conference in 1974. Right place, right time. She settled in for a long stay. Terry's story is a bit different. She came to WEWS years later to try out for Liz Richards' spot. At the time she was working a publicity job.

Morning Exchange co-host Liz Richards was leaving the show to stay home with her two young children. Her marriage to Gary Dee had been, and still is, the stuff of local legend, and that's not to mean it was positive. Late one night, Jane, who was living in Cleveland Heights, got a call from Don Webster. Jane recalls Webbie said Liz and her daughter Allison needed a place to stay for a few days, and it had to be kept it quiet. Word was that Gary had fired a shot in her direction and Liz needed a safe place to sort things out.

Gary was no stranger to firearms. When he was at WWWE, he once put a bullet into a phone book after ranting about Carl Monday.

Jane took them in. Liz and Gary eventually reconciled for a time, but the marriage eventually ended up in the courts. Liz moved to Florida, where she became an attorney specializing in family law, and she put Cleveland far behind—so far that when she was contacted about appearing on the final episode of *The Morning Exchange,* she politely declined, saying it was "in my past."

"In 1979 Liz Richards quit and they put out a call that they were doing open auditions," Terry Moir said. "A friend dared me to go to the auditions, so I sent in my résumé and got a call to come in. I went in, and they had these chairs lined up, and there are forty women there. Everyone, to a person, was either blonde or brunette, and was wearing either a brown or black suit. I had this long, curly red hair and I was wearing a blue suit. I thought, 'I'm screwed!'

"It took all day. You're moving down the line, and you go in and you see these bright lights. You know there's someone there watching you. Joel Rose did the interview with me, and he asked me all these outrageous questions. He started out with, 'Do you have a boyfriend?' 'Not right now.' He asked, 'If you had a boyfriend, would you have sex with him?'" Not your average interview questions, but keep in mind, this was Joel Rose.

After the interview process Terry got into her little yellow Chevette and went to her parents' house. "I was devastated. It could not have been worse. I had bought a new blouse and looked at the sleeve. All the tags were still on it!"

It obviously could have been worse, but Terry came through okay. "I sat down and wrote a letter to the station about how it was like being in a beauty pageant, and you're Miss Bolivia, and you don't speak English. Two days later, I got a call from Carol Story. 'We got your letter, and we want you to come back.' I went back several times, and it went from forty to twenty to fifteen to five, and I was surprised I was still in. But while I was going through it I learned what the producers did, and I thought I could really do that! They had all the power, and the talent did what they were told! Jan Jones got the job, but I talked my boss at Case Western Reserve University into putting a TV on my desk so I could try to figure out how to put doctors on the *The Morning Exchange, The Afternoon Exchange,* and the Channel 3 show. My job was to get people in the newspapers, on TV, and on the radio."

A friend who was an associate producer at *The Morning Exchange* told Terry she was leaving for Chicago, and to call Jane Temple. "When she asks how you know about the job, just say, 'Jane, good producers never reveal their sources,'" Terry explains. "I did exactly what she told me, and they had me come in that day. I was the highest paid producer they had ever hired —at $9,000 a year! I left a job making $22,000 a year for $9,000. It was really hard work, ten segments a day. It was so much fun!"

Jane remembers that hiring well: "Carol and I were beside ourselves because we thought she would be great on the air. We really wanted to hire her. The problem was that Fred was a more 'middle of the road' personality, and Joel was a snarky personality by design. We were afraid that Terry, with so much personality, would overwhelm them. That's the only reason she was not the hostess before she was the producer. When she applied for producer, it was a slam dunk!"

This was a job where you had to hit the ground running. As Terry points out, there was a pretty wide range of guests: a long line of performers from Musicarnival, the Front Row Theater, the Kenley Players, media personalities, authors, lots of local politicians, and just about anyone with an interesting story.

The Morning Exchange was not a normal talk show for a couple of important reasons: its two-hour length and the number of guests. It still holds the record as the longest running show of its time length in America. Local shows in other cities were one hour long because they were ABC or NBC affiliates and could be aired after *Good Morning America* or *Today. The Morning Exchange* started in 1972, before ABC had any morning program. WEWS ran Porky Pig and Casper cartoons from 7:00 a.m. to 8:00 a.m., which gave *The Morning Exchange* a huge lead-in. (Remember, this was before there were kid-oriented cable networks.) Long-time WEWS Program Director Gary Stark says: "Eventually we started carrying

MUST SEE APPEARANCE: *The Morning Exchange* was the place to be seen if you were promoting a product or idea. Here Cleveland Mayor Carl Stokes shares his thoughts on local politics with host Fred Griffith. *Cleveland Press Collection, Cleveland State University Archives*

the first hour of *Good Morning America* instead of the cartoons, which is one reason why it was never strong in Cleveland—because we carried only the first hour and did not clear that second hour."

The Morning Exchange ratings always surpassed those of *Good Morning America*. In the 1990s *The Morning Exchange* moved to 9:00 a.m. and the station "cleared" the second hour of GMA.

Two hours long, five days a week. That's a lot of live TV to produce. Do the math. Thirty guests per week over the course of twenty-seven years. That's a huge number, and Fred interviewed almost all of them in the way that only he could. There were a lot of fascinating people who sat on that couch. But when you're dealing with the volume of people required by the show, every now and then there would be a dud.

Terry Moir says Mark Twain would have been an A-level guest, but one Twain impersonator was anything but. "He came on dressed as Mark Twain, and he did the worst impression. He was so bad! We were trying to wrap it up, but everything reminded him of another story. He's going seven, eight, nine minutes over!" Jane brought it to an end by making a slashing motion across her throat. She recalls, "Producers were supposed to do a phone pre-interview, because there are brilliant people who are out there who are not articulate. So we always had this phrase, 'But he was great on the phone!'" There was also an African dance troupe that didn't speak English and refused to perform.

Terry recalls one guest who was not a star but who changed her life. "There was a story in *Glamour* magazine about a young woman who was from Garfield Heights and living in Florida. Sharon Komlos was married with three children and was driving down a highway in Florida. She looked over and saw a guy pointing a gun at her. Before she could step on the gas, he shot her and the bullet went into her head and blinded her in both eyes. The car stopped, she couldn't see anything, and someone came up and said, 'I just saw what happened! Let me help you!' It was the guy who had shot her! He took her into the woods, stabbed her, and left her to die."

"Sharon crawled to the highway, and a true Good Samaritan stopped. While she was in the hospital, someone introduced her to Dr. Wayne Dyer, and they became friends. I called down to Florida, and she said she knew the show because she had grown up here. We flew her up to Cleveland and booked her as the first guest, so that meant you had to be there at 7:30. I was sitting there in the studio talking to her, and she was so inspiring! I told her, 'I can't believe you're not mad at this guy!' They had caught this guy and he only got five years in jail! Sharon said, 'I lay in that hospital bed, and had to make a decision. He had taken my sight. Every minute that I thought about it, every thought that I gave him, was another thing that he took away from me. I decided that day I would never feel anger or revenge toward him because I would never be his victim again.'"

That comment really reached out to Terry. "I was at this point in my life where a lot of stuff was frustrating me and I was worried about a lot of things moving forward. I realized that every minute you think about that stuff was one more minute you took away from your life. She changed my life."

Another favorite was Richard Simmons, who was originally an exercise instructor on *General Hospital,* a very popular ABC soap opera at the time.

Jane says Simmons' Cleveland fan base was huge, and for good reason. "We would bring him to malls and get thousands of people. Someone would tell him, 'Richard, you're on.' He'd run out, pick people up, and carry them around. He bit one of the cameramen because he had a cigarette in his hand! He was crazy fun! He was a great guest, but you also realized what a good person he was, how deeply he cared for the people who loved him." Terry agrees. "The reason I loved Richard Simmons so much is because we saw a side of him that no one else had seen. He was upbeat, but he was never manic. He would go to Carol's or Jane's desk and he would take out his file box. He would start dialing numbers. 'Hi, this is Richard Simmons. I'm in town to do *The Morning Exchange.* How's your weight loss going? I'm sorry to hear that!' We had a limo for him, and his driver would take him to these different people if they needed to see him that day. He was so involved with his people."

There were also guests that went way beyond the limit, and Terry recalls the trend by then was to book unusual and weird guests.

"Phil De Marne was a producer who booked a lot of really kinky stuff. He booked a guy who had fifty piercings. I had heard about it, but at the time I was doing a lot of stuff. So we went to air and I was standing in front of the studio, and it was Fred and Lee. When it was 30 seconds out, the guy got up . . . he had a low-cut shirt so you could see his nipple piercings . . . he pulled out of his back pocket a bone and put it in his nose. Lee Jordan stood up and said, 'I am NOT on this segment!' and she walked off. So Fred was gently asking the guy about the piercings. 'How many piercings? That's very unusual.' The guy said to Fred, 'I have my penis pierced.

Would you like to see it? This was one of our many attempts to try to take on Jerry Springer and other shows. We learned a very valuable lesson, because you never did that to Fred Griffith. I answered four hundred letters by hand from people who thought we had humiliated Fred Griffith."

They laugh about it now, but Jane says it was Fred's demeanor that could often diffuse a tough situation. "I once told Fred that he was so nice to people that if he ever had Charles Manson on the show he would ask, 'And Mr. Manson, what did you mean when you wrote 'Pigs' on the door?'"

Fred really was a unique personality. Well-educated, erudite, and with a monstrous vocabulary. Terry recalled, "Fred would say, 'Why would you use a little word when a big word would do?' No one ever walked quickly. They moved with alacrity. He would always tell you, 'Don't ever talk down to this audience. They are smart people, and our job is to elevate them.' You also learned to think on your feet, and celebrities could be very demanding."

Terry's take on Debbie Reynolds was: "I remember when Debbie Reynolds was on the show. 'Miss Reynolds is here. She's in the lobby.' I went to get her and said, 'Miss Reynolds, it's so lovely to meet you!' She said, "Thank you, Dear. Where's your makeup artist? I really need someone to look at my face.' We didn't have a makeup artist! I went in to Carol Story and asked, 'What are we going to do?' Carol walked into Fred's office, took his coat off a hook, and there was a smock under it. She put it on and said, 'Don't worry about it.' Then she walked out and said, 'Miss Reynolds. Hi, I'm Carol. I'll be taking care of your makeup.'"

The Morning Exchange offered a lot of useful information, but it still came down to entertainment. Terry says, "Every year that I was there, we did an April Fools' show. They were not real guests, but we would never tell Fred, Jan, or Joel. By the second time we did it, they obviously knew. One time, Joel dressed up as an old woman who could read pirogies and we took live calls. 'What is your name? Jenelle? Jenelle, pick a number between two and seven. Oh, the pirogies are telling me a lot.' Dick Urichak and Bob

Seeley were the Smith Brothers, who had invented cough drops. Once the crew did their take on Jazzercise, but they did it with beer. They would chant, 'Three, four, five . . . and drink.' Fake guests for the entire show."

Back to the real guest. There was more than one adult claiming to be the kidnapped Lindbergh baby or Princess Anastasia from Russia. And then the ultimate horror to anyone with a live show: a guest armed with an f-bomb! A super right-wing-type crusader came on *The Morning Exchange* to rail against immorality in media, and he meant all media. TV, movies, and that filthy rock and roll radio. Then he spelled out the f-word. Joel Rose congratulated him: "As a born-again Christian, you've become the first person to ever use that word on our air!"

He wouldn't be the only one on Cleveland TV. Years later, WJW was covering the annual Christmas tree lighting at Public Square. Santa Claus would be pressing the button, signaling the start of the holiday shopping season. He walked onto the stage "Ho, ho, ho-ing" all the way, tripped, fell, and broke his wrist! Santa also had an open mic nearby and let out an "f-bomb"—but he didn't spell it out. Moms across the Square became human earmuffs for their kids.

Another *Morning Exchange* moment: The anti-porn crusader who brought a briefcase full of smut and freely waved it around, live on the air. Bill Baker would later say you had to book a "freak a week" if you wanted to be a successful show. There was no shortage of freaks.

The Morning Exchange was also about lifestyles. People did care a lot for soap operas, and no one knew more about them than Lynda Hirsch. Plus, she was funny, could ad-lib like a champ, could fill in as a co-host, and had a personality that made you feel like she was an old friend living right next door. She joined *The Morning Exchange* in 1976 and stayed for six years, then returned in 1988 until the show shut down production.

The format was proving to be a monster. At one point Fred Griffith did double duty, also hosting *The Afternoon Exchange* which ran from 1977 to 1982 (when it changed suddenly into *Live on Five*). *Afternoon Exchange* was popular with viewers, but not necessarily with the critics. The *Plain Dealer*'s James Ewinger claimed the expanded news was more packaging than substance, and pretty much just teasers for the 6:00 p.m. newscast. He said it was more small-scale duplication of the news than expansion.

The competition, WKYC's *5:30*, didn't excite him either. Ewinger said it had "all the panache of a how-I-spent-my-summer-vacation essay. There is little entertainment or information, but it sure does take up space." He seemed to like Mona Scott, but still didn't think her personality was right for a news show, even though it seemed to work on *5:30*. Simeon Smith, not so much. He warned Channel 3 to sedate him "before his hyperactivity rattles the show right off the air." *5:30* would eventually fall by the wayside.

Other stations had let WEWS take the risk, but when they saw *The Morning Exchange* take off, they tried to get a piece of the ratings pie with their own live shows. WKYC gave weatherman Bob Zappe a shot with *Zap*, a show he co-hosted with Nancy Glass. It was taken off the air after a brief run. Then Channel 5's Dave Patterson went to WKYC for a Phil Donahue-type show, but even with Al Roker as an occasional fill-in host, *The Dave Patterson Show* went belly up. In 1983, Channel 3 took a chance on its own talk show, *AM Cleveland*, with Scott Newell as the host.

Channel 3 was aggressive in the war against *The Morning Exchange*, even running a snarky ad in a July 1985 *TV Guide* with two mannequins sitting at a table and a headline that read, "*AM Cleveland* is up against some pretty stiff competition." This in spite of the fact that, as television writer Maria Riccardi pointed out, WKYC had actually tried to bring Fred Griffith over the year before.

Some considered *The Morning Exchange* to be too laid back. That same month, the show brought in new blood with Randi Hall replacing Jan Jones as co-host.

On-air personalities are driven by their own motivations, and managing them can be difficult. That job belongs to the executive producer, who has to tell on-air personalities that their hair isn't right and that their last interview 'wasn't punchy enough' while still reassuring the star that he or she is doing a great job. It's a delicate balance.

"A lot of the people in sales really liked Randi Hall," Jane remembers. "Randi not only was good-looking, smart, and capable, but she had that special spark with the camera. Jan Jones had it. Robin Swoboda had it. Whatever it is, Randi had it."

"She was great on air—and effective with guests and sales alike—but she slowly alienated people because she'd never settled into Cleveland; she was in a commuter marriage, traveling weekly from Cleveland to California." On one particular day, Jane recalls, "I told Randi that we were going to tape a Thanksgiving show. Good news: You get to be away for Thanksgiving. Bad news: You've got to be in town the weekend we're taping. She hit the ceiling! She said I hadn't told her, and said she did not have to do anything I told her."

Don Webster, the assistant general manager, stepped in to mediate the standoff. Jane recalls, "Webbie called Randi into his office with me and a couple of other people and said in so many words, 'You cannot treat people like this. If Jane tells you this is what you're doing, you have a responsibility to do it.' Randi anticipated that she was probably going to be fired if she stuck around. She got up, went to the door and said, 'You know what? I'm gonna make this easy on everybody. I quit!' She slammed the door and walked out."

"A few months later, I was doing a spot in the studio. Jim Knight walked in and said, 'Tell me, why was Randi Hall hired instead of Lee Jordan?' (Lee had been the runner-up when Randi was selected.) They hired Lee that day, and she's been there ever since."

AM Cleveland gave *The Morning Exchange* a pretty good fight. Lynda Hirsch went over to Channel 3 for a time and brought a legion of fans with her. That helped push *AM Cleveland* to beat

The Morning Exchange from May 1986 through February the next year. Then Fred and the gang rallied, and when WJW began airing *Sally Jesse Raphael, AM Cleveland* eventually settled in at number three and WKYC looked at its options. The final *AM Cleveland* show was set for March 31, 1989.

It boiled down to economics. You had to look at how much the show cost to produce versus how much it brought in. The key female demographic was fading, and *The Morning Exchange* had a steady share of those still watching. Common sense tells you that number one stands to bring in a lot more cash than number three, and number three didn't seem to be going anywhere. Plus, NBC wanted its stations to produce programs that could be farmed out to other stations. Syndication meant revenue flow, although station management said that didn't influence their decision. It just made more sense to replace Newell and company with *Hart to Hart* reruns, at least until they found something else. That was pretty much what happened to Patterson's show. If you don't have enough people watching at that hour, it's not cost effective.

The show went out with a bang, though. Producers reunited a mother and her forty-two-year-old daughter whom she'd given up for adoption. Al Roker offered his condolences from New York, and co-host Kim Scott handed out copies of her exercise video. Then she asked if she could keep a copy of "Dr. Ruth's Game of Good Sex" that had been left over from a trivia contest.

Newell did an exit interview with *The Plain Dealer* and said the criticism the press had given him had really stung. One called *AM Cleveland* "bland" and described Newell's "blinding Close-Up smile." Another said he was hyper, bouncing off walls. Newell would go on to other TV jobs here and there, and in 2015 he was stringing locally for the Weather Channel.

The Morning Exchange, even though it was ranked number one, had to deal with many of the same issues. In December 1989 the station gave Joel Rose his walking papers. The show was going back to a two-host format, and that was one salary saved. After two decades at WEWS, Rose said, "It's a real disappointment to me. It's kind of like somebody dying." On the other hand, Channel 5 welcomed back Lynda Hirsch with open arms. She replaced another soap expert, Gary Warner, who had commuted from New Jersey to do his segments on Channel 5. When Lee Jordan signed on, it was a pretty smooth transition. Lee and Fred made a good team.

The Morning Exchange was synonymous with WEWS. It was a brand name with a built-in fan base. *The Afternoon Exchange* took off right away (and there was even a clone, *The Fairfield Exchange*, which went on the air in 1982 in southern Connecticut).

Channel 5 tried expanding the show to Saturday and Sunday in 1995 with *The Weekend Exchange*. It was strictly interviews and was hosted by Leon Bibb. Despite Leon's eloquence and interview skills, *The Weekend Exchange* went south the next year (and Leon made a smooth transition to *Kaleidoscope* with a similar format).

There's a long, complicated story about what led to *The Morning Exchange*'s demise, but let's just sum it up this way: Changing time slots, the push by ABC for Channel 5 to air the full two hours of *Good Morning America*, the emergence of *Live with Regis and Kathie Lee*, and fewer stay-at-home moms. Syndicated shows were proving to be very popular. At one point, WEWS put the half-hour *Martha Stewart Living* in the middle of *The Morning Exchange*. Some viewers thought it was a really long segment in *The Morning Exchange*.

It was also getting tougher to book guests. Politicians didn't want to risk lengthy interviews, stars didn't tour as much, preferring satellite interviews if they were plugging something. Plus, the audience had become a bit jaded—*show us something new*. And it was getting harder to find something new.

Eventually, loss of audience and competition from syndicated shows proved too much. By 1998, the show was revamped into *Today's Morning Exchange*. Fred Griffith had been reassigned as a field reporter, and former WJW anchor Robin Swoboda was on the set with weatherman Mark Johnson. It just wasn't working anymore, and Channel 5 pulled the plug on September 10, 1999.

The final show was like a family reunion with past co-hosts and producers coming back for one last time.

There were also some odd moments. Cleveland Mayor Mike White stopped by to give a proclamation to Fred, and then broke down into phony sobs. As he departed, White said with a smile, "And they say I don't have a sense of humor." Joel Rose opened his shirt to show a tee shirt that said, "Will talk for food." Champagne corks popped, balloons dropped, and then goodbye *Morning Exchange*.

Fred Griffith would go to Channel 3, Lee Jordan and Mark Johnson stayed on a 5, and most would live happily ever after.

Most, but certainly not all.

"You can never wipe out a sex scandal"

The Strange, Sad Saga of Joel Rose

JOEL ROSE KNEW HOW to push buttons. Sometimes he would say or do things and then stand back and watch the reaction. You could get into a discussion with him taking the most outlandish stand and still everyone would part with a smile. But what he did on the morning of August 4, 2000 is still being debated.

Rose created a character for himself that wasn't too far from reality. Bill Barrett at the *Cleveland Press* called his on-screen persona, "a gimmick, the ayatollah, the Grumpy in a nest of Happys like Don Webster." He left TV in 1984 and returned to radio. Then, suddenly, his life started to come apart.

On Wednesday, August 3, 2000, there was a knock on the door at Rose's house in Brecksville. Cuyahoga County sheriff's deputies and police from Cleveland Heights and Parma had a warrant to search for evidence, and this was very serious business. They took a computer hard drive, a typewriter and a Titan .38 caliber handgun, and then told Rose he was coming with them. Not to jail—there hadn't been any charges—but to Parma Community General Hospital for samples of saliva and body fluids. There were traces of both on postage stamps and items mailed anonymously to as many as thirty-two women in Northeast Ohio. The packages had been sent from post offices and contained panties, pornographic magazines, and typed greeting cards, often with very graphic messages. When Rose heard the allegations, he quickly denied them.

The accusations were very troubling. Pandering obscenity and menacing by stalking were very serious, although, again, no charges had been filed up to that time.

Packages had turned up on doorsteps in Cleveland Heights, Parma, Brecksville, Lyndhurst . . . ten cities in all. When they arrived, many of the recipients went right to their local police, who had since been comparing notes and working on the case for two years.

Not all were convinced Rose was behind it. Brecksville Police Chief Dennis Kancler said, "I cannot believe it. This man is committed to community safety." Most of the Brecksville cops knew Rose. He had an interest in ham radio and was a part-time consultant for the department. Earlier in the week, he had helped install a new communications system for the fire and police departments. Rose would even volunteer for the city's Home Days.

But there were plenty of people who did think Rose was the culprit.

The evidence was disturbing. Lingerie was a common item included in the packages. A woman in Mayfield Heights received a leopard-skin teddy with a typed card that was signed from an "Admiring Friend." She told postal inspectors, who said, "Welcome to the list!" A Brecksville woman found a manila envelope in her mailbox with an orange blouse and a pair of mesh panties. There was also a note that read, "I have pictures of you." In Lakewood, a woman had been getting the packages for more than a year and had simply handed them over to police. One had blue silk lingerie wrapped around a white plastic vibrator, and another woman got a nightshirt with two holes cut in the chest and a threatening message written on it. All were disturbing.

Some were downright terrifying. A former TV reporter got a package at her home on Valentine's Day . . . with no postage. It must have been hand-delivered. She told investigators she had broken out in a cold sweat. The packages that had been mailed had been sent from Hinckley, but had a phony post office box as the return address. No fingerprints were found on the packages.

One woman reportedly quit her job because she was terrified the sender would track her down, while at least one other invested in pepper spray and a cell phone. Some would later say

THE ULTIMATE DECISION: Joel Rose's friends defended him for many years after the TV host took his own life. The debate over his possible guilt continued as well. *Cleveland Press Collection, Cleveland State University Archives*

they checked the back seats of their cars and worried about possible sexual assaults against themselves or their families. Some notes mentioned family members by name, including husbands and kids. At least ten women pursued counseling.

Most of the victims were blond and thin, and they now shared something else: fear. *The Plain Dealer* reported that the packages were often very explicit. There were often mailed around holidays, and in some cases continued to arrive for as long as two years. Several went out on Valentine's Day, and one woman reported a card that had come right out and stated the sender looked forward to having sex with her. That one, like others, was accompanied by panties.

A special investigator started calling the women to say they weren't alone. Some of the victims of the mailings formed a support group to compare notes and share them with investigators. About a dozen gathered at a Parma courtroom to share their experiences over coffee and doughnuts. There was a questionnaire asking where they shopped and what restaurants they frequented, and whether they had ever been targeted this way before. All of the targets seemed to have a connection with Cleveland radio and TV and covered a pretty wide age range, from college students to women in their sixties. One told *The Plain Dealer* she had been a frequent guest on *The Morning Exchange* when Rose co-hosted. She received the first package in January 1999. That one had an orange blouse and black mesh panties, and packages after that had more lingerie and dresses and very disturbing notes: "I have a picture of you," "You have beautiful legs," and "I'm enjoying your flirtations." The woman said she was afraid to check her mail, especially around the holidays.

Investigators came up with three possible suspects: an employee at a local TV station, a media freelancer, and Rose. The first two were investigated and ruled out. At least one of the victims had confronted Rose to ask if he was the culprit. Rose denied the charge.

As part of the investigation, detectives starting picking up Rose's garbage from the tree lawn. Rose thought something was fishy when his trash bags were missing and the neighbors still had theirs on the curb. He asked Mayor Hruby if he had any idea why that was. At that point, Hruby knew Rose was being investigated, but also knew Rose had applied for an overseas communications job. He told Rose it could have been the CIA.

Then the police came calling.

After being escorted to Parma Hospital by the police, Joel Rose headed home. He decided to stop in at the Cleveland Heights police department to retrieve his handgun. The gun had not been used in connection with a crime, so they gave it back to him. Next,

Rose bought a new computer to replace the one that had been seized as evidence. When he finally got home, Rose got a call from his best friend, Merle Pollis. The two had been a point-counterpoint duo on radio for years, with Rose being the conservative and Pollis the liberal. Rose said he'd like to discuss the case with Pollis, but had been advised by his attorney not to say anything. He would only say he would be proven innocent.

Word got out that *The Plain Dealer* was going to run a brief story the next day and was preparing a more in-depth article. Rose told his family he was being framed. As soon as the story broke, things might get very ugly, very soon. Rose's attorney, Gerald Gold, later told a reporter he called *The Plain Dealer*'s Rosa Maria Santana in an attempt to hold the story. "I told Rosa the whole thing was absurd. I told her there were no charges for Joel to respond to. What could he say? 'I didn't do what?'" Gold thought he had convinced the reporter, but he hadn't; the story broke the next day.

Rose knew what was coming. That Friday morning he woke up early, and at about 6:00 a.m. he told his wife, Lois, he was going out for the paper. The small headline in the Metro section pretty much said it all: "Ex-TV Host Under Investigation in Porn Case."

There were no eyewitnesses to what happened next, but this much is certain: Rose walked into the woods near Glen Valley Drive, put his .38 handgun to his right temple, and pulled the trigger. Lois found the body shortly afterward.

Rose left behind four notes on top of the morning paper. They were addressed to his wife, his stepdaughter, Brecksville Mayor Jerry Hruby, and the police chief. The contents were kept confidential, although the recipients told newspaper reporters that Rose had proclaimed his innocence in all of them. Reportedly, the note to Chief Kancler stressed that DNA evidence would vindicate Rose.

Many of Rose's friends remembered him as someone quite different from the man under suspicion. Former WEWS news director Garry Ritchie didn't believe the claims against Rose. Merle Pollis said it felt as if someone had cut off his right arm. "I can tell you that no one was more incredibly loyal to his friends." He added, "I hope he's not just remembered for this. I fear that will be the case, but I pray it's not so."

The public's reaction was immediate, and much of it was directed at *The Plain Dealer*. Rose's suicide got a lot of ink that Saturday. It was obviously front-page news, but there was also an editorial stating: "A troubled man has left us in a troubling way." It also pointed out: "No good could come from his death. If he was responsible for the pornographic parcels, he has forfeited the opportunities for redemption that this life can offer."

Then *Plain Dealer* writer Sam Fulwood III came to the paper's defense. In another piece he wrote that dozens of phone messages and e-mails had been directed to the paper's newsroom, and most blamed its coverage for Rose's suicide. Reporter Rosa Maria Santana got more than her share, with one caller accusing her of having blood on her hands and signing off with, "I hope you're happy." That one really affected her. She told Fulwood, "I didn't cause his death. It was incumbent upon me to write about an investigation that I learned about. I'm just the messenger." Fulwood agreed.

"Reporters did not start this investigation. It started because a number of women reportedly received packages from Rose containing underwear and pornographic magazines. They were scared; in some cases, terrified. They were victims," Fulwood wrote. He also pointed out: "Journalists have only credibility to sell. If enough people decline to buy, then we're doomed."

The media took its shots, too. Joanne and Anna Wolper asked in *Editor & Publisher*: "Did the Cuyahoga County prosecutors tell *The Plain Dealer* that they could get the DNA test results within forty-eight hours, as they told us? Did the editors or reporters ask how long it would take to get those results?" MediaNews.org quoted *Chicago Sun-Times* editor Phillip Blanchard: "I'm sick and tired of amateurs screwing up my business. I'm also weary of paid apologists attempting to justify irresponsibility."

Scene quoted a longtime friend of Rose, psychologist Dr. Michael

Leach: "Either Joel was a dirty old man, more than anybody ever knew, and that having somebody discovering it was too much for him to take, or he was being accused of awful crimes in *The Plain Dealer* for which he felt there was no defense." That same article pointed out the criticism the *PD* was getting for using anonymous sources, and the paper was accused of "practicing tabloid journalism to outright murder."

But *Plain Dealer* editor Doug Clifton defended the coverage, saying the paper would do it the same way if it happened again. He pointed out that newspapers often write about ongoing investigations with no charges filed, but added another important point: Despite the use of anonymous sources, the story was backed by a five-page probable cause affidavit that had been sealed by a judge, which served as the basis for the search warrant. Clifton said, "I felt confident that we had knowledgeable, authoritative law enforcement sources from multiple jurisdictions confirming for us the nature and scope of the investigation." *Scene* mentioned that Clifton had argued that "Rose simply didn't protest loudly enough when he was contacted by the paper about the charges." That didn't wash with some people, including Rose's daughter, Lauren Reed, who said, "I can't believe he himself believes that."

The *Free Times* opened up on Clifton. In an article titled "Questionable Ethics," writer David Morton stressed that *The Plain Dealer* couldn't be blamed for Rose's suicide. He also speculated that the newspaper's staff had to be troubled by that outcome, but also pointed out that the way the paper reported the story had raised "an ethical debate among people in media circles." It also quoted that same article by Phillip Blanchard: "The wording of the story, as any Journalism 101 student could tell you, essentially convicted Rose on the basis of an anonymous accusation. Any editor who signed off on that story needs a spell in re-education camp."

Clifton came right back at them. In a later issue, Morton described *The Plain Dealer* as in "full spin mode," and revealed an email given to him by Rose's best friend, Merle Pollis. It was a response sent by Clifton to Pollis six days after Rose's death.

Morton interpreted the email as saying Rose's decision to end his life indicated his guilt. In part, Clifton's email read: "I know how I would react to a false accusation of that sort. It would not have been to blow my brains out. On the contrary, it would have been to LOUDLY and vigorously to deny it and to sue the newspaper for libel and the police for malicious prosecution." He pointed out that when *The Plain Dealer* had asked Rose for a response, he had said, "I couldn't comment on that," which Clifton said was hardly a ringing denial. The email ends with these words: "I'm sorry Mr. Rose took his own life. He no doubt would have done the same thing when it became fully public by whatever means." As Morton put it, that was an assumption of guilt and that Clifton was implying that Rose's suicide had been inevitable.

In that same issue of *Free Times*, Morton wrote in his article "Loose Lips" that a question remained as to who had tipped off *The Plain Dealer*. "We are forced to ask who's hiding behind the mask of anonymity. Did these sources stand to benefit from Rose's embarrassing exposure?" He speculated it could have been a cop in one of the twenty-four different police departments involved in the investigation. But Morton also suggested, "The most reliable and likely source of information would have been within the Cuyahoga County prosecutor's office." He speculated that office would have had "powerful motives" for leaking the story to the press, including getting more people who had received similar packages to come forward.

Letters poured in to *Free Times* about the case as well. One defended *The Plain Dealer*, saying anonymous sources were commonplace and even that paper used them now and then. On the other hand, another reader brought up that anonymous sources run the risk of credibility. "How reliable is the information, and where did it come from?" the writer asked. That same writer called out *The Plain Dealer*: "Journalists aren't supposed to identify suspects in a crime by name until they have been arrested." He pointed to the case of Richard Jewell, who had been suspected, though never charged, in the Olympic bombing in Atlanta. The local newspaper put him on the front page, and Jewell said his life became miserable after that.

Merle Pollis was quoted: "Joel really cared about his reputation. You can never wipe out a sex scandal. There was nowhere for Joel to go."

So why was Rose even suspected in the first place? There were clues that seemed to point in his direction, but Cuyahoga County Prosecutor Bill Mason added a new twist: Rose's own website. Mason told *Editor and Publisher* that Rose became a "hot suspect" because the site was the home of the "Briarhop Corners Bulletin," a satirical monthly e-newspaper with characters like Lyle "Snappy" Purvurt. He was described as a staff photographer who stole women's underwear that was drying on clotheslines. The satire was taken down after Rose's death, but a few were kept by recipients. One showed a good example of Rose's unique humor.

"Hulda-Marie is an assistant nurse's-aide dietary assistant at the Briarhop Corners Retirement Community. She says the part of her job she likes best is cleaning up the patients on chili dog night.

She enjoys her other duties as well, she says. 'We have a little game we call hide the rectal thermometer, we give clues and the aides have to guess which patient it's hidden in. The winner then gets a Bud Light.'"

Almost two weeks passed. The DNA results were in, and the tests could not link Rose to the mailings. Plus, in a separate report, it was shown the typewriter that had been seized did not match the one used to write the suggestive notes. Even so, with no DNA evidence, Rose was still considered a suspect in the investigation. As DNA expert James Wooley said, "It just means the guy didn't lick the stamp." If it had been someone else's DNA, it would have been considered vindication for Rose.

Merle Pollis had a theory about who was behind the mailings, but wouldn't share it. He would only say his sources didn't implicate his old friend.

Bill Mason's office had no other suspects in mind, but still asked a forensic psychiatrist to review the evidence and come up with a psychological profile. *The Plain Dealer*, WEWS and other news organizations sued to see the contents of the sealed affidavit, but prosecutors argued against that move, in part to protect the victims' anonymity. After Rose's death, one of the women said for the first time in two years she went out to get the Sunday paper without looking around first.

Whatever the circumstances turned out to be, the bottom line is that a number of people could be considered victims of the scheme, including one who paid the ultimate price.

News, Views, and
Loose Screws

Tv NEWS IS ONE tough business. Not so much reporting the news, but giving viewers a reason to tune in in the first place. Especially now. The Internet changed everything. Young viewers want instant access to information and see no reason to wait around until 6:00 p.m. to see a story when they can pull it up on their cell phones. In fact, most stations will say they program for TVs, computers and phones . . . as if that's going to bring in younger people. They're competing with on-demand video, streaming video, and any number of other reasons not to switch on the old set at home.

It wasn't always that way. Sure, there used to be a lot of competition—with radio and newspapers—but video won out and TV stations had their hands full giving the audience something they couldn't find down the dial. Here's the problem: There's only so much news to report, and stations started adding more programs to get a jump on the competition. News departments also have a lot of overhead with big salaries and equipment, so they have to generate a lot of revenue just to break even. Cleveland tends to be pretty traditional and even conservative when it comes to watching news, so when something different comes along, it can be a huge success or go south pretty quickly.

In late 1969, WKBF took a chance with a ten o'clock news program, but even with a tiny staff, it drained enough money to put the station under. When WUAB started news at ten, it took a chunk of the audience and it was a four-way battle with WKYC, WEWS, and WJW. The competition changed again in 1994 when the Fox network bought WJW. The station switched networks with WOIO, Channel 19, which became a CBS affiliate. Now linked to the "Tiffany network," WOIO had plans to set up a news department that would be distinctive but still worthy of the CBS brand. One programming suggestion, though, would not have fit that mold in the least.

Mike Drexler had been a long-time news voice in Cleveland on WERE, and that's where he met the infamous Gary Dee. Gary was one of the first shock jocks, and he helped define that role every day on WERE and later on WHK. Gary left Cleveland in the 1980s for other markets, but hadn't found the same success elsewhere. So the "Mouth of the Cuyahoga" came back looking for a gig.

Drexler had an idea for a daily program called *News, Views, and Loose Screws*, and it pretty much lived up to that name. He thought it was a perfect fit for WOIO. The idea was for the show to open on a dark stage with a spotlight shining on a bar stool. Drexler would come out with a handful of scripts and do five minutes of traditional news. Maybe one line about what sports team was in town or who had won the night before. Then it was on to gonzo news with cameras all over the city recording people's opinions about news events, and maybe even some live segments . . . which in that format would have been like playing Russian roulette.

The plan called for a stripper in a bathing suit to roll around on the weather map on the floor. "It's going to be HOT in Warrensville Heights tomorrow." You get the idea. The program would end with Gary Dee's remarks on the day's events in a way that only Gary could do it. WOIO did launch its news department, but without Gary, the stripper, and the rest.

A personal anecdote from Mike Olszewski . . .

Malrite Broadcasting left the radio business to concentrate on its TV stations. I really liked the way they operated, and when the opportunity came up for a gig at WOIO and WUAB, I put in my notice at the radio station. WMMS did a lot of cross-promotion with WOIO when they were both owned by Malrite, so I pretty much knew half the staff already.

The Rock and Roll Hall of Fame was getting ready to open in about a year, and I'd been following that story since the mid-1980s. This was going to be a spectacular TV event, so the time seemed right.

We had almost a year to plan, but covering the Hall wasn't any easier on TV than it was on radio. Milton Maltz was the man in charge at Malrite. Early on, he saw the cultural and economic impact the Hall would have on Northeast Ohio if Cleveland got the nod. Plus, the whole region would get a lot more positive attention and help shake off the rust belt image . . . but you had to land the project first. Other cities had some pretty impressive credentials and could make a strong argument for them to get the Hall.

Here's what Cleveland had: Alan Freed and the Moondog Coronation Ball, the aborted show that had given rock and roll an instant reputation for being "dangerous." It also sold more records per capita than any other city in the country, and that was based on strong radio, like WHK and WIXY.

When FM took over in the late 1970s, WMMS stood head and shoulders above all the other stations. It was a ratings monster and a promotional machine that could mobilize huge crowds of people. Even though just about every station in town worked to get the Hall in Cleveland, don't think for one minute that we would have stood a chance without WMMS.

Yet that presented a problem for us at WOIO.

Milton Maltz sat on the planning board and knew everything about the project. He was also sworn to secrecy, was a man of his word, and wouldn't tell you anything if you asked him point blank. That also meant if you missed a story about the Hall, and that rarely happened, people wanted to know why.

It took a long time for the Hall to finally break ground, and the grand opening was going to be huge, with international coverage, and Cleveland was going to shine. WOIO ran stories every week for a year, and was even going to suspend some of its programming to carry the opening live. Local Hall officials would hold regular briefings to update the media, and at one of those mid-summer meetings, they were asked how much access local press would have to the Hall on opening day.

"None, unless you're an inductee!"

Whoa! What was that? They were expecting so many people and so much attention that only national press and the folks inducted into the hall would be allowed in the first day? This was troubling news. It was time to get very creative!

Our coverage was going to be for TV, but our mentality had to be more like WMMS—rock and roll. In the back of your head you thought, "If I can't do it, they'll find someone who can." You didn't say, "I can't do this." The proper response was, "How can we do it?" I'd been around the music industry long enough to know that trends come and go, and when you're no longer pumping out hits for the record company, you're on your own. There were plenty of people in that boat. We needed someone who looked great, could think on their feet and get the nod from the Hall.

It didn't take long to find her.

Mary Wilson was one of the original Supremes, and I'd met her a few years before when she was promoting her autobiography. She wasn't doing as much since Diana Ross left for her solo career, so I contacted her through a publicist and asked, "How would you like to be a TV reporter in Cleveland?"

There's something else to keep in mind. By 1995, there had already been a lot of people inducted into the Hall, and they couldn't fly every one of them in for the grand opening. (In fact, on the day of the event, Dion DiMucci was seen watching the opening from the crowd—no one had really noticed him.) This was an opportunity for Mary to do something new, maybe use it to launch her own TV career—as well as enjoy the opening. She said, "See you in Cleveland!" We had a plan, but we didn't tip our hand.

The station had some other irons in the fire. One of the original MTV jocks, Nina Blackwood, was from Northeast Ohio and she joined WOIO's coverage. But there were some folks the station had to pass on. John Sebastian had been inducted into the hall with the Lovin' Spoonful, but he was a little expensive for our budget.

Another former Clevelander, Casey Kasem, who had worked as "Casey at the Mike" on WJW-AM, was willing to come in for the event, but he needed support with him at all times, including a makeup artist.

One insider we had in place was WOIO engineer Brian Panek, who had taken a part-time production job working the huge concert scheduled for Municipal Stadium that weekend. He fed us videotape of the rehearsals, but the station couldn't really use it because it would have been obvious where it had come from.

On the Friday of the grand opening, just about every radio station had set up remotes for their morning shows at the parking lot near the Hall. It looked like a gypsy camp, with tents and trucks everywhere. Since I'd been covering the Rock Hall from day one, I was asked to appear on most of the shows, and just went from table to table. Brian called the videographer to say he had a copy of the artists and songs that would be featured at the show that Sunday. This was a major scoop, and there was plenty of top-secret info. It showed Bruce Springsteen and the E Street Band joining Chuck Berry for "Johnny B. Goode," and later the Boss and his band backing up Jerry Lee Lewis for a medley of his hits, Little Richard playing "Long Tall Sally" with Jon Bon Jovi, Bob Dylan, the Allman Brothers Band, and the list went on and on. It was a step-by-step blueprint of the concert, and it was about to discreetly pass through hands to the folks at WOIO.

Brian said he would be able to sneak away for a few minutes to pass it on, but he stressed we had to keep it very low-key. I was waiting to go on WMMS when I noticed Brian crouched down, waving me over to the back of the tents near the Coast Guard station. Just as he was handing over the production book, one of the jocks yelled out, "Hey Olszewski! What are you doing back there? A drug deal?" Everyone stopped to stare at Brian and me holding the book between us. We were like deer staring into head-lights, but at that point, it didn't matter. We were ready to roll.

When Mary Wilson arrived, she made it clear that she was there to work. She started by singing "Stop! In the Name of Love" live on the noon report with Romona Robinson and Jack Marschall, and she was introduced as one of our guest reporters. That also meant the other stations weren't about to interview someone giving exclusive reports for a competitor.

You couldn't stop her! Ask the videographers, Jim Jackson, Scott Wallace, Roger Lumpkin, Tim Jenkins, Frank Wiewandt. When Mary was done with one report, they took the tape back to the station and she worked on the next.

The Rock Hall lived up to its word: only inductees had access. But that included Mary Wilson. Not only was she an inductee; she had also loaned her stage gowns to the Hall for its inaugural showing, representing a significant part of the Supremes display in the Motown exhibit. Now, though, she was traveling as part of a full TV crew. Along with a cameraperson there was me, a field producer and a bodyguard, Greg Mayo, who kept the fans at bay while Mary worked (although she always made time for them). This was a situation the Rock Hall didn't expect.

We came in through the front door—the other stations didn't seem pleased—and went to the exhibit hall. We were told, "Sorry, you can't come in!" but Mary didn't blink. "Hi! I'm Mary Wilson of the Supremes, and I'm here to check on my gowns in that exhibit over there. Two key words: *my gowns.*" The Hall set the rules, but they couldn't say no.

There were plenty of inductees in the Hall that day, and Mary knew them all. Smokey Robinson, Martha Reeves, James Brown . . . they all lined up for an interview with the newest TV reporter in Cleveland. Same thing happened at the formal dinner that evening. This woman didn't stop! She was twice as old as some of the videographers yet three times as active.

Then we had to deal with the concert.

This was easily one of the biggest concerts ever, and security was extremely tight. We managed to get backstage access, thanks to Mary, and, true to form, she started getting interviews right off the bat. One of the folks who ran up to say hello was "Little Steven" Van Zandt from Bruce Springsteen's E Street Band, who was also a fan.

"Hey Mary! You gonna be doing some Supremes stuff?"

She explained that the trio would be represented, but that without Diana Ross, there would be no Supremes reunion and the Hall had opted to have Melissa Etheridge sing "Love Child." Steven did a double take, but didn't miss a beat. "Then you're singing with us!" Mary didn't want any awkward moments, thanked Steven, and said she was only there representing the TV station. Then she got back to work doing the interviews. But that's where we hit the wall.

HBO had exclusive rights to the concert, and back then, portable TV cameras were big and heavy. You couldn't miss them, and the producers didn't miss us. After a couple of interviews, security rushed up, separated us from Mary, and quickly showed us the door. They also demanded the tape. I knew Ed Louloudis was a great videographer, but I didn't realize how talented he was with sleight of hand. He went nose to nose with them, exchanged a few heated words, and then snapped, "All right, dammit!" and he handed over a tape. A blank tape! Ed had discreetly pocketed the other one, and we were off to the station with another exclusive. Mary called us to ask what had happened, we thanked her for all her hard work and said, "You are now officially free to enjoy the weekend." She laughed and said, "I already have!"

Mary and I crossed paths a couple of times after that, and she fondly remembered her busy weekend in Cleveland television.

Every news department has a few stumbles now and then.

WOIO shared a news team with sister station WUAB, and there were some top-flight journalists ready to take the challenge. But there were plenty of good journalists at every station, so 19 needed something different. You have to keep in mind that in 1994, the Internet was in its infancy and most homes still didn't have computers, so TV was still the place to get breaking news.

City News in Toronto was high-energy and innovative, with videographers coming in off the street, plugging in raw tape and showing it as they described the event. The anchors were more likely to sit on top of the anchor desk than behind it. That might have been a bit too different for folks in Northeast Ohio, so the station decided to do a sort of hybrid, combining some of those new ideas with more traditional news. They designed a round news set for Channel 19 that insiders called "the hot tub." Now all they needed was the heat.

Denise Dufala came over from WJW and was paired with Emmett Miller, who had the news anchor look. The station also hired former Miss America Gretchen Carlson for its weekend anchor. You had Dave Barker from Los Angeles, Amy Castelli from Pittsburgh, Ben Holbert, a Cleveland news veteran, and the list went on from there. Sure, there were some growing pains and even some victories, but the progress was slow. WOIO was up against four stations with long-established news departments, and viewers are creatures of habit. They return to the same stations they're comfortable with, at the same time every day. But management wanted ratings, and keep in mind that this was Malrite, so they expected results now. Greg Caputo was the news director, and he had done pretty well in his previous gig in Cincinnati. Cleveland was a completely different market with its own unique personality, and Caputo found that out the hard way.

In November 1995, the Ohio State Buckeyes were preparing for their annual match-up against their arch rivals, the University of Michigan Wolverines. Now, remember that this was a much looser newscast, but "loose" is a subjective term. Denise Dufala had graduated from OSU, and former WMMS-FM morning man Jeff Kinzbach was a University of Michigan alum. Kinzbach was now on WWWE-AM, and the two kept up a long-standing tradition of betting on the OSU-Michigan game, with the loser getting a pie in the face. That was not a good year for Ohio State, which lost to Michigan, 31-23. Dufala was set for a whipped cream facial.

She let Caputo know that she had arranged to have Kinzbach and his co-host Ed Ferenc stop by to give her the pie live at the end of the newscast. Caputo strongly nixed the idea, but it didn't stop

HEAVY IS THE HEAD . . . Gretchen Carlson
was crowned Miss America 1989, but her reign
as Denise Dufala's co-anchor was short-lived.
Miss America Organization

there. Some calls were made and word came down that not only
would Dufala take a pie in the moosh, but here would be a small
clock in the corner of the screen during the news showing how
many minutes were left in the broadcast until she got it!

Here's the rub: The newscast that night was pretty typical:
murders, violence, tragedy . . . and a clock showing how many
minutes until the anchor went slapstick. When the clock ticked
down, Dufala put on a poncho, whipped cream flew everywhere,
and—whether it was his move or not—Caputo didn't stick around
much longer. It should be pointed out that Greg Caputo continued a long and very successful career in Boston and other major
markets, retiring as news director from WGN in Chicago in 2014.
You just didn't hear much about his time in Cleveland.

Oh, and Emmett Miller. Emmett left WOIO for parts in movies such as *Wag the Dog* and *Inferno* and hosted his own syndicated series about the paranormal, *Strange Universe,* before returning to the news anchor desk at KTLA in Los Angeles. After Cleveland, "La-La-land" didn't seem quite as crazy.

By the way, another local news anchor was linked to the paranormal before coming to Cleveland. Tim White was an accomplished journalist and media relations expert when he hosted the nationally syndicated UFO show *Sightings* on the Sci-Fi Channel from 1992 to 1997. He left that show to take over the anchor desk at WKYC. It seemed like a natural transition.

"We're number three!"

Getting Into the TV News Biz

IF YOU DON'T HAVE a revenue flow, you don't have a TV station. Management is always looking for a new way to bring in cash . . . or at least not lose it. Six years before WOIO took the "news plunge," its sister station WUAB decided to test the waters. Local news was bringing in $13 million in advertising to the three established stations. WUAB thought it could take $1 million of that in the first years. Some saw it as a gamble. Others thought it was foolish.

Planning started in mid-1987. WUAB had been around for almost twenty years when the station's owner, Gaylord Broadcasting, decided to finally pull the trigger and do a nightly newscast. A ten o'clock newscast. It could be risky. The old Channel 61, WKBF, had tried a bare-bones ten o'clock 'cast, and that had helped ease the station to oblivion.

News is expensive. Gaylord had deep pockets, though. They invested $2 million in a proposed hour-long, Monday-through-Friday newscast. It would be the only hour-long local newscast in Cleveland. They called it "traditional news at an alternative time." But viewing habits are very hard to change. They had a huge job ahead.

Work began on building sets and a newsroom at the Parma studios. Computer equipment was installed, and the station signed on with the Cable News Network for anything that wasn't local. Then they had to hire a staff—and who's going to sign on with a first-timer? Surprisingly, they managed to assemble a fairly strong line-up. Dan Acklen had produced the 6:00 p.m. 'cast at WJW. He told *The Plain Dealer* that at one time he had suffered from "affiliate arrogance," believing that independents would go down in flames. Part of it was from budgets, and most independents didn't have them. Most independents weren't owned by Gaylord Broadcasting.

Anchor teams are like the front cover of a magazine. You need something—or, in the case of TV, someone—to catch the eye. Agents came calling, ads were placed, and tapes were reviewed. Seventeen hundred people applied for twenty-five jobs. As many as fifteen applications were from local news people at other stations who wanted a shot at the anchor desk. The station eventually hired Romona Robinson and Bob Hetherington as their two leads. Substitute anchors were Jack Marschall from WEWS, David Lane from Buffalo, and Mary Ann Herman from Columbus. Ben Holbert had worked radio at WJMO, and he was welcomed to the fold. But these were, for the most part, new faces, so you needed someone who screamed out familiarity. Then the seas parted and in walked . . . Gib Shanley on sports!

This was a coup. Shanley was a legend at WEWS, and people still recalled his burning the Iranian flag on-air. He was never afraid to share opinions, and now WUAB give him that opportunity. The cornerstone was in place.

Acklen seemed pretty confident. He told *The Plain Dealer*, "The world is different now. At one time people were trained to watch the affiliates, so they watched Walter Cronkite and the eleven o'clock news. But with twenty-four-hour cable, more radio, videocassette recorders, and time-shift viewing, people have gotten a little out of their viewing habits. And the networks have seen an erosion in their share (of the audience). Cable doesn't have local news, and that's where we fit in."

Did he remember what had happened to Channel 61? Sure, but Acklen stressed that Gaylord had plenty of money. He pointed to the recent sale of its Tampa station, which had brought in $365 million. Even so, the station was betting that some people wanted to get to bed early and a ten o'clock newscast would get them there quicker.

He might have been on to something. That same article pointed to Portland's KPTV, which beat two out of three competitors with

SHOW TIME: Romona Robinson had a big job ahead when WUAB named her co-anchor of the *Ten O'Clock News. Cleveland Public Library*

its ten o'clock show. General manager Marty Brantley said his success was linked to the fact that: "The baby-boom generation is getting older, and since women have become a major factor in the workforce, fewer people are home to watch the news at six. Sometimes the 10:00 p.m. newscast is the first full newscast they get to see." Plus, big-money advertisers like banks and car-makers advertised on newscasts, and an earlier program was an attractive proposition.

Keep in mind that an hour newscast is a lot of time to fill. Acklen promised a lot of relevant content, "hard news with lighter moments. Not feature laden." Plenty of in-depth stories, too, but he also warned you have to face facts. The likability issue was usually the deciding factor. He said the other stations would have a lot of the same stories, but "what makes the difference for the viewer is the look of the station, the feel, the comfortability factor with those anchors. The final choice is who you like."

The kickoff date was set for January 4, 1988.

Did they really think they could pull any audience from the

big three? Apparently so. They started out thinking a three-point rating would put them in a pretty good position. Soon they were talking as high as a nine-point rating that would nudge WKYC, which was in third place at that time.

Part of it came from the lead-in programming. *Shaka Zulu* was doing pretty well on Channel 43, and the audience might be too lazy to get up and change the channel. At last they hoped so.

There were plenty of dress rehearsals, lots of meetings, and then finally the premiere came and went. The next day it was like waiting for a review of your Broadway show. It probably wasn't what they had expected.

The Plain Dealer used the words "flubs" and "weak writing" . . . in its headline! It didn't get much better from there. The paper called it a "strained newscast." Columnist Debbi Snook wrote: "Tongue-tied moments, vacant pauses, and mispronunciations littered the station's first broadcast of the *Ten O'Clock News* last night, creating enough awkwardness to nearly topple any sense of professionalism the station was striving for." Snook noticed some missed cues, even mentioning the anchors leafing through scripts on camera when Romona looked up and said, "Bob?" She also pointed out weatherman Frank Cariello rocking back and forth in his chair, and holding scripts in the final moments of the show. Gib Shanley got high marks, so high that he might have put his co-anchors in a bad light. Finally, as the newscast drew to a close, Hetherington teased a story "you might not see on other stations." Turns out the story was congratulations from Mayor George Voinovich for giving Cleveland an earlier newscast. Snook ended the column saying after six months of hype, even one scoop would have been nice.

Here's something a lot of people didn't realize. Channel 43's news team was at a disadvantage. The location behind Parmatown Mall had formerly worked fine for the station, but it wasn't ideal for a news department, which has to mobilize on a moment's notice. The neighborhood had seen a lot of growth in twenty-five years, and besides mall traffic, there were a lot of restaurants at Ridge and Ridgewood Drives. Add to that nineteen traffic lights between the station and the Ridge Road exit to I-480. They weren't synchronized, and Parma city officials said they didn't have the money or police manpower to have someone direct traffic at rush hour. It was a disaster during the Christmas shopping season. Acklen said there was talk about a downtown bureau. It was clear that 43 would have to do something if it wanted to cover breaking news.

To be fair, opening night is where you see the most mistakes. The ten o'clock newscast continued to improve in both quality and ratings. When it finally overtook WKYC in 1992, members of the staff ran through the halls at Channel 43 chanting, "We're number three! We're number three!"

You think it's a gamble starting a newscast? Try starting a whole TV station. Ask the startup crew over at WBNX. In 1985 it was set to be the fourth independent TV station in Northeast Ohio. The Reverend Ernest Angley bought the station in 1982 for $2 million from his fellow evangelist, Rex Humbard. It had a big signal, 2.35 million watts, and that meant everyone would see it. So, what would they see?

Angley was no stranger to TV. He bought time for his *Ernest Angley Hour* in one hundred twenty markets, including Channel 43 and Akron's WAKR. Even when Angley's new station got off the ground, WUAB would still carry Angley's show as long as he paid the bill.

It was a sure bet that WBNX would have some sort of Christian-based format, but management said that didn't mean "hell and brimstone" from sign-on to sign-off. There were plenty of old movies and TV series. Here's the problem: The older they were, the more affordable they were. Christian Broadcasting network did the same thing. Lots of religious programs, and then on to *The Many Loves of Dobie Gillis* and *Wagon Train*.

No one seemed worried about competition from WBNX. Jack Moffitt, the general manager at WUAB, said, "They'll probably go after low-cost programming we're not interested in." You could see why he thought that way. At the time rights for a show like *Cheers* went for $30,000 an episode, and you bought the whole syndication package. Moffitt thought WBNX would be bankrupt if it went after a hot series like *Webster* that was just coming on the market.

Over at WOIO, general manager Dennis Thatcher asked the same questions. He told *The Plain Dealer*: "How can they generate that kind of revenue? I don't think they'll have a significant effect on the marketplace."

Your revenue flow was linked to your Arbitron ratings, and it took a while to crack that egg. New stations had a big job ahead. Thatcher's station carried another religious program, *The 700 Club*, and as he put it: "Let's face it, they're not world-beaters when it comes to ratings. To make a dollar impact, you need ratings." The program director at Channel 61, Jerry Kerwin, echoed that. Before Cleveland had cable, the old WKBF, now WCLQ, tried a subscription service showing first-run movies in the evening. The picture was scrambled, and you had to rent a Preview decoder to see the films. That went south pretty quick, and in late 1983, they went back to free programs, the kind that needed advertising, and 61 was struggling like everyone else. Kerwin said, "Most of the kind of programming they (Channel 55) will have is not ad supported." Media buyers at ad agencies didn't have much faith in their chances, either.

There was also an elephant in the room called cable television. It was already starting to make its way into Northeast Ohio, and that was the biggest competitor for everyone. WBNX went on the air, signed on with reruns, local programming, and even some syndicated shows. Let the battle begin.

But then something changed. Warner Communications' WB network eventually settled in at Channel 55 and brought in huge numbers with young viewers. The money demo! The WB became the CW, same programming and same demographic, with *Gilmore Girls, One Tree Hill, Smallville,* and plenty more. With no news department to drain its revenue, WBNX became a major player on the local TV scene.

Sometimes you gamble. Occasionally, you win!

"You'll be lucky if any of you leave my office with a job!"

Channel 5 Reports the End of the *Cleveland Press*

THERE'S PLENTY OF NEWS on television, and it seems like there's more every day, even if there's nothing happening. The glut of TV news programming we have now might hinge on an incident that occurred in late 1980.

The *Cleveland Press* had been one of the most influential papers in the country. It resurrected Houdini's career with a series of front-page stories debunking psychics across Northeast Ohio. It essentially put Sam Shepard behind bars after his wife was murdered in 1954. It could be a king-maker in local and state politics. That was the influence of its long-time editor-in-chief, Louis B. Seltzer. Then, after a long career, Seltzer retired in the mid-1960s, and soon afterward the news business itself headed into a major transition.

Afternoon papers like the *Press* were losing readers, and *The Plain Dealer* surged ahead. A slumping economy didn't help. The cost of publishing the paper, competition from other media, and declining revenue from ad sales put the *Press* on the ropes. When union contracts came up for negotiation, it was going to be a battle.

A lot of folks thought the *Press* was already doomed. Scripps-Howard owned the paper and wanted concessions, but the unions were standing firm. The impending death of a major newspaper was also a huge story in Cleveland and across the country. TV took the ball and ran with it, but it wasn't going to be easy.

Eric Braun had a long-standing reputation as a topflight reporter in radio when he switched to television and signed on at

WEWS. He produced the eleven o'clock news and did some street reporting, and knew how important the *Press* story was. Here's the problem: WEWS was owned by Scripps-Howard, the same company that owned the *Press*. Scripps wasn't tipping its hand, meaning Channel 5 had a big job trying to cover the story.

Don Robertson, a long-time columnist for the *Press*, wasn't afraid to speak his mind and was loyal to the unions. Cleveland was a blue-collar town, and Robertson got a lot of popular support. Here's the hook. Robertson also had an evening talk show on WERE, the news and talk radio station where Braun had previously been news director.

Robertson invited officials from the *Press'* unions on-air to talk about the negotiations, and they described the situation as dire. Eric heard the show and raced with a video crew down to the radio station at 13th and Chester. Members of the negotiating committee told him confidentially that Scripps had demanded concessions and had given them a deadline to meet their demands or the paper would likely shut down operations. The union guys likened it to a gun to their heads. But the talks were continuing, and they didn't want to jeopardize their position. That meant they wouldn't go on camera. So for the TV crew, now what?

Eric described the conversation as a "gold-plated source," but he still needed pictures. He worked with a pretty savvy videographer named Mike Ward, who would later become WEWS' assistant news director. Braun and Ward put their heads together and came up with a plan to stress the importance of the talks. They took the live broadcast truck to the front of the *Cleveland Press* building at East 9th and Lakeside. It had a sandstone façade with a bas-relief image of the Scripps logo, a lighthouse, which was the same one seen on "Wooz." (That's what the folks at Channel 5 called the station, pronouncing the call letters, WEWS, as a word.) There were no lights on that part of the building, but Ward set up a 500-watt lighting rig on a portable generator and they were ready to roll. Eric did his live shot standing in front of the image, told what he could, and ended it this way: "The *Press* unions have seventy-two hours to accept the concessions . . . or this lighthouse could go dark forever." At that point, Ward cut the lights. Very dramatic, good TV . . . and they sure didn't expect what happened next.

Remember, these were the days before everyone had a cell phone in his pocket. Sixty seconds after the report aired, the newsroom contacted Ward by radio to say, "Mr. Perris wants Eric to call him at home. Immediately!" Don Perris was the president of Scripps-Howard Broadcasting (sister company to the *Cleveland Press's* ownership), and he was enraged. Eric described his mood as "incandescent", and Perris demanded everyone involved in the story, including the news director Garry Ritchie and the station's vice-president, Ed Cervenak, be in his office at 8:30 the next morning. He ended the phone conversation screaming, "You'll be lucky if any of you leave my office with a job!" Needless to say, some folks at WEWS didn't get much sleep that night.

Ritchie and Braun spoke by phone close to midnight. Ritchie wanted to establish before their meeting whether Eric was sure of the story, and the answer was "yes." Even so, there was a lot of tension as they filed into Perris' large office on the third floor of WEWS. Perris was slouched behind his desk as the three managers filed in, and Eric recalled his mood was now "apoplectic."

It turns out, after the report aired, Perris called Jack Howard, son of the founder of Scripps-Howard, at his home in Cincinnati. Howard was privy to the contract talks with the *Press'* unions. He chose his words carefully, but did say the company was "playing tough" with the unions. Perris had apparently been kept pretty much in the dark on the corporate side. Yeah, the story was on the money, but Perris said the crew might have "stepped over the dramatic line" in the way it was reported. That was it. Phew!

Eric not only survived, but would eventually become the station's news director.

We know what happened to the *Press*. In late 1980, Cleveland businessman Joe Cole bought the paper after the unions agreed to concessions. They tried putting out a tabloid and Sunday edition,

CHANGING OF THE GUARD: News director Eric Braun's inside tip on the closing of the *Cleveland Press* opened the door for more TV news at WEWS. *Eric Braun*

with lots more color, and even morning delivery. It just didn't work.

On June 17, 1982, Eric Braun, who by this time had been promoted to news director at WEWS, got a call from one of the paper's columnists, Harriet Peters. She said an emergency meeting had been called for the staff that morning in the city room. Most expected "Taps" to be played, followed by distribution of pink slips. It was over for the *Press*.

Afternoon Exchange had been on the air at Channel 5 since late 1977. A clone of the very popular *Morning Exchange*, it ran from 4:00 p.m. to 5:00 p.m., and was populated with authors, feature stories, and some brief news headlines. There were celebrity interviews, movie reviews, Lynda Hirsch talking about soap operas, cooking demonstrations—you get the picture. It was essentially a local magazine show.

Then at 5:00 p.m., you had Merv Griffin, who sang a few songs with Mort Lyndsey and the band, and at 6:00 p.m., the station switched over to news. The *Press* folding its tent would make headlines nationwide, and Eric knew that the story should be on the air through the afternoon. But there was no real news flow from 5:00 p.m. to 6:00 p.m. He approached the station's program director, Gary Stark, with a proposal he knew Stark wouldn't like.

Stark did all the syndicated buying for WEWS, and programs like *The Merv Griffin Show* generated revenue. Eric explained that the station had been covering the story since late morning, and it was important enough to give *Merv* the afternoon off. The station had its live trucks ready to roll, and reporters were on the phone, lining up guests like former *Press* editor Louis Seltzer. The conversation went back and forth, with Perris and Cervenak joining the debate. The decision was made to pre-empt *Merv*, and WEWS was on the story like ugly on an ape. Kudos poured in about the coverage. And that gave Eric some leverage to try a new idea.

In 1982, Cleveland was the eighth largest television market in the nation, and one of the few where local news had not already expanded into the 5:00 p.m. hour. Braun pointed out to station brass that the news transition drew an audience, and this was the moment to shake up the schedule. "If Cleveland doesn't have an afternoon newspaper, we can be the replacement!" he argued.

Local stations in New York, Philadelphia and Detroit already had early afternoon newscasts on the air called *Live At Five*. The sales department was consulted, and they agreed that the changes made sense. *The Merv Griffin Show* was moved to 4:00 p.m., and because of WEWS's dial position, the preposition was changed and *"Live* On *5"* was born.

The other stations took note, and it wasn't long before WJKW and WKYC jumped on the five o'clock bandwagon.

So you think there's too much news on local TV? Perhaps you can thank the *Cleveland Press*.

Happy Talk and Hair-Dos

The Never-Ending Search for Viewer-Friendly Faces

Tv NEWS MADE ITS first real mark in November 1963. Up to that point radio and newspapers were the top news sources, but live coverage of the Kennedy assassination put us on a new course. It happened so suddenly that most TV news departments weren't ready to exploit the change. In fact, most just tweaked here and there when possible to see what worked and what didn't. By about 1970 it was becoming more of a science.

The *Star* was one of Cleveland's underground newspapers, and in 1974 it talked about the trend to treat news as show business. It noted that one of TV's biggest assets was accessibility: "Convenience is the mother of popularity." The most important stories were pretty much dropped in reporters' laps instead of their having to hunt through the newspapers for them. Plus, video was a huge draw, especially in the sixties when civil rights, the cold war, politics and so many other issues made for better stories with moving pictures.

Production became a lot more streamlined, and there was plenty of content, too. The number of stories became a drawing card. More reports in a half-hour newscast meant less time spent on each story. Local TV news was essentially transformed into a headline service. That placed more emphasis on the personality of the people who brought us the news.

Doug Adair had made his mark at WJW with the chemistry he shared with co-anchor Joel Daly. Other markets saw how well they interacted and an offer came in from Chicago's WKBT (which would become WLS-TV) asking both to come to the Windy City. Adair stayed behind, but Daly headed west.

Adair made the move to WKYC in 1970 for an eye-popping $65,000 a year and was paired with Virgil Dominic. Some folks called what Daly and Adair had at Channel 8 "happy talk," but WKYC's news director Richard Lobo preferred to label it "controlled informality." Whatever it was, Lobo wanted it in his newscasts at Channel 3. It wasn't long before Dominic got a huge offer in Atlanta, and Adair was flying solo. But station management now had a different way of looking at things, and they wanted things to look "pretty."

The search was now on for "viewer-friendly" faces. That meant new roles and less face time for vets like Wally Kinnan, the Weatherman; Paul Sciria; Del Donahoo and others, although Donahoo would later get some high-profile roles on the road and the WKYC morning show. The *Star* had predicted a similar fate years before at WEWS for Bill Jorgensen, who landed a gig in New York, and Tom Field, who ended up in radio and doing aluminum siding commercials on TV.

By the mid-1980s it was hard to keep track of who was on what station. As *Plain Dealer* TV critic Maria Riccardi pointed out, you would see anchor Susan Howard and reporter Dale Solly on Channel 8 one day, and Channel 3 the next. (Solly would later say his tenure at WKYC may have been shortened by a live report he did on a Shaker Square event promoting the campaign to bring the Rock and Roll Hall of Fame to Cleveland. He was an accomplished guitarist, going back to his days at Bedford High School. After he interviewed former WHK jock Johnny Holliday and some other folks at the site, he jumped on stage to tear it up with the house band. Solly did some posturing and made a few faces and was told when he got back to the station that management didn't appreciate that part of the report.)

All the stations had people moving in and moving on. Then Tana Carli took the local TV business in a whole new direction.

It was late summer 1981, and Judd Hambrick had left the WJKW anchor desk to start his own production company. Who was going to fill the chair next to Tim Taylor? Five staffers at Channel 8 auditioned for the job: Dale Solly, Susan Howard, Barbara Geddie, Kathy Adams, and Tana Carli. Carli was the former Miss Ohio who dazzled audiences with her accordion playing in the 1980 Miss America contest (she came in second). No one thought she had much of a chance at the anchor job because she was only twenty-five years old, with about a year of consumer reporting under her belt, when she tried for the job. Her degree was in accounting, not journalism. The serious money was on the other four.

That was a bet you would have lost.

News director Virgil Dominic told *The Plain Dealer*'s James Ewinger, "It all came down to gut instinct. We thought the time was right for a woman anchor, and the chemistry was right between her and Tim." Ewinger also stressed that Carli's appointment was part of a new trend in local TV news. Forget experience. It was about physical appeal, and that went for men and women. As he put it, "Face it, there are not many gargoyles working before the cameras these days." To her credit, Carli would later admit that Dominic hadn't hired her for her journalistic experience because, as she acknowledged, she had none.

The next day *The Plain Dealer* ran an article saying it was more than gut instinct that had landed Carli the gig. Anonymous sources at Channel 8 revealed she had been chosen by a focus group, the "Faceless 100," working with Research Center Incorporated out of Lincoln, Nebraska. They showed tapes of the finalists to one hundred people from outside Northeast Ohio so they wouldn't be affected by the "used to" factor. They wanted them judged on believability, communication skills, and audience appeal, not familiarity. That went against what Virgil Dominic said, or at least played a much bigger role.

Then general manager Bill Flynn chimed in, and he wasn't happy: "People in Lincoln, Nebraska? I made Tana Carli an anchor!" When he was asked how much the research had influenced his decision, he barked, "What you're asking are personal questions and, frankly, you are wasting my time and yours!" That didn't sit well with Ewinger, who ended his article with, "If

THE POLKA QUEEN OF TV NEWS: Tana Carli took her accordion skills from local talent shows and beauty pageants
to the co-anchor's job at Channel 8. *Cleveland Public Library*

Channel 8 puts that much stock in appearance, physical appeal,
and potential, at the expense of proven news-gathering skills, then
maybe the viewers should pay attention to some other newscast,
assuming the other stations are not playing the skin game." Ouch!

Carli knew she and other female anchors were under a microscope. She told *The Plain Dealer*'s Barbara Kingsley, "Every person
is waiting to prove she's a bobblehead. When she makes her first
mistake, they say, 'I knew it. She's stupid.'" Carli also said a focus
group once said she seemed like a pretty good reporter, but also
that "she dresses so well. It looked like she had stopped in after a
night on the town."

Six months later, Ewinger likened Tana Carli to the "Eva Peron of local television." He said that, like Peron, Carli had come out of nowhere, worked in the shadows for a time, and seemingly overnight made $60,000 a year as a major market news anchor. Yet viewers were indeed coming back to Channel 8! Ewinger said he wasn't alone in his skepticism, and "our short-sightedness is our albatross."

Carli anchored at Channel 8 for a while, but left for Miami to get married and eventually do some acting. Sandy Lesko jumped from WEWS to WJW, and scores of names like Wayland Boot, Joe Conway, and others stayed for a time and moved on. This doesn't reflect their credibility; Riccardi correctly points out that it came down to perceived likability.

In 1982, enter Denise D'Ascenzo.

WJKW signed on D'Ascenzo out of St. Louis by way of Syracuse. News director Virgil Dominic was traveling to Montreal when he had a layover in New York state. He was channel surfing and saw her doing the weather. He later told *The Plain Dealer*, "She imparted her information with a good deal of simplicity so it was easily understandable." And let's face it, she looked good on TV—and had really big hair.

Folks in the front office at Channel 8 saw the hair, too, and it wasn't long before some of the other female anchors were "Denise-ified." Sandy Lesko started to look a bit different, as did Loree Vick, who Riccardi says took on a different vocal inflection as well. She would later call Vick a D'Ascenzo clone. After a time, the consultants tired of the big, curly hair look in favor of a one-length, traditional bob. In the news business, it's known as "the cobra."

Oh, and Denise D'Ascenzo? She was only in Cleveland for about four years before moving on. For months there were rumors that she was ready to exit, then in August 1985, she told station management she'd be gone by the end of the year. As she put it: "A lot of Hail Marys went in this." She was only twenty-seven and engaged, and she missed her fiancé and family. She didn't have to worry about a "non-compete" either: There was a clause in her contract that allowed her to leave if she got married.

Hair became an important factor. A 1987 *Plain Dealer* report quoted an unnamed but respected news veteran who said, "If there is a hank of hair hanging in the middle of your forehead, the audience will watch the hair and not hear one word of what you have to say about the national debt." That same report pointed out that until Channel 3's Doreen Gentzler changed her hairstyle to a "wind-whipped, frosted, and sprayed affair," she was the only female anchor in town whose hair actually moved.

Gentzler's hair was a hot topic from her first day on the air. She kept tacked to her bulletin board a slightly crumpled piece of stationery that had been sent in by a viewer. It included two newspaper pictures of Gentzler, and the woman who sent it in had erased the anchor's hair and drew in the style she thought she should wear. Problem was, it looked like Betty Boop! In the margin the viewer wrote, "Improvements." This might have creeped out most people, but Gentzler said the content of the note and the penmanship made it look very innocent.

Doreen Gentzler had the TV look, but Channel 3 had hired her for her reporting skills and on-air style. She was later described in a newspaper report as looking "young, upwardly mobile, with a medium-tough veneer and a friendly, no-nonsense delivery. Not only appears to be professional, but also seems to be a human being."

She had every intention of staying in Cleveland, too. She got married here and liked the city and her co-workers a lot. What she didn't like was working at the last-place station in town. Gentzler couldn't give a reason for the revolving door at the station or its inability to get any numbers. She said, "Smarter people than me haven't been able to figure it out for years now." Plus, she wasn't all that confident about the Cleveland TV market. Gentzler said "it lacked sophistication and competitiveness," and she didn't under-stand why the big three news departments at that time weren't fighting tooth and nail over the top stories. She laid part of the blame on the lack of newspaper competition after the *Cleveland Press* went south. Gentzler was also disgusted with the long line of interns who were more interested in anchoring than sharpening their anchor skills. She wasn't alone.

This was a problem facing the whole industry. You only had so many jobs, and the "newbies" didn't want to wait for the top spot. Dick Tuininga at Channel 5 said he was concerned by kids getting out of college communications programs with anchor-level dreams and entry-level skills. Even today, so-called broadcasting schools are pumping out graduates who hit a wall and end up in sandwich shops. Those alleged schools aren't cheap, either.

Back to Doreen Gentzler. There were also questions about a Channel 3 management decree that she give a "softer and warmer delivery" when she was partnered up with Judd Hambrick, who had returned to Cleveland television. Gentzler said, "I have one act. It's the same act I have when I'm with friends, the same act when I'm arguing at the grocery store, and the same act when I'm on the air." In 1987, she decided to take "the act" on the road to Philadelphia and eventually, Washington, DC.

Most people who were convinced to come to work in Cleveland actually liked it after they arrived here. The reasons they left were usually very interesting. You remember John Hambrick at Channel 5 in the seventies, the first of brothers to work in local TV. Dan Coughlin had worked with him from 1989 to 1990 at WCIX in Miami, many years after Hambrick had left Cleveland. This was some station! Other staff members were John Roberts and Gisele Fernandez who would go on to CBS, Bill O'Reilly at Fox. Big names, and at that time, Hambrick was bigger than all of them!

He never slowed down. He would do interviews on the street in Spanish and translate them for the viewers. Dan had a small refrigerator under his desk, and on Fridays, the crew would get together to crack open a few beers after the show. Dan says, "One night John admitted that he had made a lot of money in television, but he considered his only real success was in Cleveland." So why did he leave? "John said, 'I would drive in every day from Shaker

CLEVELAND IS GREAT . . . BUT IT'S TIME TO MOVE ON: Doreen Gentzler was described as "upwardly mobile," and she left WKYC because Channel 3 News couldn't get out of the ratings basement. *Cleveland Public Library*

Heights and head into town on Chester Avenue. For six months, I did not see the sun.'" It was time to head south.

Now, here's something to keep in mind. While the stations were profiling potential anchors, they had to match them up to the "Cleveland personality." And what was that? Kristin Ostrowski was the news director at WKYC in 1983 and summed it up this way: "Cleveland wants warm and friendly. The girl next door. The guy down the street. They don't want uppity; they don't want sophisticated. They want friendly and approachable. They don't want wimps. Cleveland is a blue-collar, beer-drinking town." That could account for the infamous WEWS news promo with Gib Shanley as a pro wrestler!

Still, fair or not, you still had to have a TV look. In the Old West they had six-guns in their holsters. Now they had hair spray, and it didn't hurt to be young and perky.

Remember Christine Craft? Back in 1983 she won $500,000 in an age and sexual discrimination lawsuit against a Kansas City, Missouri, TV station that had demoted her from news anchor to reporter. She argued that the station cut her because they didn't feel she was attractive enough and not deferential to men. By the time Judd Hambrick had returned to TV news at Channel 3, he started raising eyebrows with some of his comments regarding Craft. He told *The Plain Dealer,* "Stations hire anchors who make people feel comfortable. It's the height of absurdity that she could sue and collect on the same principles on which she was hired. Any anchor who enters the business not believing looks and communication skills are what makes or breaks you should be doing voice-overs for nursery rhymes for a toy company." He went on to say, "I don't think society is ready for an all-woman newscast. I might be wrong. You have to do whatever the public wants. It's a mass medium."

There's more. He said, "If the audience wants an all-male anchor team and the general economy dictates that, that's just the way it is. Those are the basic business tenets. People might cry and moan and sue, but the public can change its mind when it wants to." Granted, that was in the 1980s, but it's not likely that Hambrick would be invited to keynote the National Organization for Women convention.

The superficiality was frustrating, especially for people trying to show they had the chops. TV-3's Anne Mulligan said she would put everything into a story, but people would call in to say they liked her clothes, and asked where she got her hair cut. She said, "I feel like throwing the television at them!" Mulligan was also the first to say that she didn't get hired at her first job a few years before at Channel 8 for her background in TV journalism. After college she decided to train horses and went fox hunting. She tried modeling, and when that didn't work out the way she had hoped, she started looking for other options. Mulligan met Channel 8's Dave Buckel and Mike Keen at a fashion show, and set up an audition at the station. She was hired as a reporter-trainee and shortly afterward, got the reporter's gig. She thought it was because they "needed a blond, Irish-Catholic girl" and considered herself a "cosmetic hire." Mulligan auditioned in other markets, but hit a wall. She said, "Youngstown didn't even want me as a weather girl!" She lucked out with Channel 8, but it took a while for the audience to warm up. Some old ladies wrote in to say she was "pleasant and serene." Another guy asked her out on a bowling date, and not because of her journalistic skills.

There's another side to this story. Anyone who knows Lynda Hirsch will tell you she is one of the brightest, funniest, most sincere and sophisticated people you will ever meet. Everyone from media celebrities to the average person on the street will tell you the same. When she started out as TV-5's soap opera critic they wanted her to be a "character anchor." Big hats, blowing bubbles, the feather boa. Kind of a stereotype, and definitely not Lynda Hirsch.

She went to WKYC for a time and had to undergo some extensive facial surgery by her own choice. It was actually a medical decision. One day a colleague from WKYC was speaking to a women's group, and Lynda's name came up. A woman told the speaker she liked Lynda better when she was less attractive! The speaker said, "But she's so much happier the way she is now." The woman's response? "So what?" Nice lady!

Let's get beyond appearances. Over at WKYC, news director Ron Bilek didn't seem impressed. The joke was that Channel 3 was battling the Cleveland Indians for the most last-place finishes, and Bilek came to WKYC believing "(The newscasts) all have the same flat look, the same flat feel." He said, "This town five years ago was star-studded with talent. Now, there are no real personalities here. Somebody has got to figure out what it is that can make them a little bit different, and we're all angling for that." Let's face it. This guy had his hands full, and he didn't want to be called to the woodshed by Channel 3's general manager Neal Van Ells. No pressure there!

That didn't seem to faze Bilek. He told Riccardi that even he wasn't sure what the viewers wanted. "We're after something that I can't quite explain," he said. But he didn't exactly endear himself to the staff at WKYC when he said, "No one shines. It's all just old-time. They just blob along." Blob along?! There's more. He told *The Plain Dealer*, "You have to get an act people buy. No matter how good our talent thinks they are, they're not good enough. The folks out there are not buying them, hook, line and sinker." He made other comments to *The Plain Dealer* that raised eyebrows, but not ratings.

By 1984 Ted Henry was already a name at WEWS and on his way to becoming an institution. After his co-anchor Pat Minarcin was given his walking papers, Henry was the solo anchor at Channel 5, and was one of the first to seemingly undergo "Koppelization." No, not the Alfred E. Neuman hair cut that Ted Koppel wore (although you might see the comparison), but the way he conducted interviews on ABC's *Nightline*. Henry would swing around in his chair to show the back of his head while he interviewed a guest or reporter on a big screen. All the stations did it. *The Plain Dealer* pointed out that the backs of Tim Taylor's, Judd Hambrick's and Henry's heads were becoming as familiar as the front.

Henry actually got good press. A *Plain Dealer* report said he "looked hungriest for news. Part of it could be body language, the way he sometimes leans into the desk, but another part is his phrasing—tight, short, and effective." The paper also pointed out what it called Henry's excesses. "He oozes with so much sincerity, it sometimes seems like he's selling it." Well, the results certainly sold commercial time.

TV news producers wanted viewers to feel as if they were in the anchor chair. WEWS news director Dick Tuininga said the anchors should become "an extension of the viewer. It gives a feeling of immediacy . . . Hopefully, Ted's questions are very close to what the viewer would ask from his family room."

An annoying trend that is still with us today was including live shots just for the sake of having live shots. Riccardi said the practice was aimed at showcasing reporters, putting them on the scene of an event to show they were digging for news first hand. It was pointed out that those live shots often put solid reporters like Paul Orlousky or Dale Solly on dead-end streets doing reports long after the actual event had occurred. Bilek defended that: "You're out in the community, you're out where the people are." Or were, at least . . . some time earlier.

(A side note: Live shots could be frustrating. Stations paid a lot of money to have their graphics wrapped around the news van, so producers were under pressure to include a live shot every newscast to justify the cost—even if there were no real reason for a live shot. They could be dangerous, too. Once, in later years, when a shooting happened in one of the city's poorer areas, a homeowner charged the WOIO news crew, screaming they only came to his neighborhood when something bad had happened. Tough to argue that. The crew got out as soon as it could.)

There were flaws in relying heavily on live location shots, which Bilek acknowledged at the time. Some reporters could pull it off, but others couldn't. "When you do live badly," Bilek said, "what you show people is that you have lousy people doing it. That's the problem. We have to work on that as an industry."

Bilek did say something that few could argue with. The consultant at Channel 5 was quoted as saying news writing needed improvement. It needed to be more conversational, talking to the viewers, instead of down at them. Competitor or not, Bilek agreed, "A lot of times we come off as preaching. We're trying to do something about that."

One thing that didn't really change that much was the video. Pictures sold the story, as they had for many years. Back in 1964, when teenager Beverly Jarosz was murdered in her Garfield Heights home, the TV stations showed graphic scenes of the blood-spattered bedroom. It was shot in black and white, which only made it slightly less shocking, but it did get a reaction from the public. *The Plain Dealer* and the *Cleveland Press* did their part to exploit the story, and cops were posted on the side street where the killing had happened to handle all the traffic from curiosity seekers checking out the crime scene.

Keep in mind that a major turning point in the effort to end the war in Vietnam came with gruesome footage on the nightly network news. That happened just about every night. At dinner time! Was that what the viewers really wanted?

Later, even the "happy talk" formats could still use stories with "blood, gore, sex, and fluff," according to one *Plain Dealer* article, which also pointed out that news executives "sometimes can't resist the good footage that comes with gore."

In May 1984, *The Plain Dealer's* Tom Brazaitis decided to check out what viewers thought about controversial content on the airwaves. He visited the Federal Communications Commission in Washington, D.C. to look over the correspondence from Cleveland. The files were actually pretty thin. Apparently a lot of folks didn't know or care that they could complain.

The biggest gripe was not about violence but was about sexual content. A man in Parma said he was disgusted that one of the story lines on *Dynasty* centered on two gay men and "not a bit of remorse!" Another viewer in Solon vented over a *Real People* segment about a bartender who mooned his customers while mixing drinks. Then there was the guy in Lakewood who was watching the play *The Best Little Whorehouse in Texas* and was embarrassed when his kid asked what a whorehouse was. Now, if he knows the name of the play and his kid is in the room . . . never mind.

Local news and infotainment took a hit, too. A viewer in Ashland County wrote, "I watched with amazement and disgust as (the host) interviewed the author of a pornographic publication, *How to Satisfy a Woman Every Time and Make Her Want More.* Rest assured, I will not watch Channel 5 in the future, nor will anyone else I can influence." Apparently he believed he had more influence than he really had. A few days later, his wife wrote in on the same stationery complaining that she was "viewing Channel 5 . . . Fred Griffith was flashed on the TV screen and made this announcement. 'Watch tomorrow's *Morning Exchange* and find out how much sex activity is normal.'" She went on to say, "Discussing this pornographic subject matter under the disguise of public service is unacceptable. Because I am a mature adult, I can deal with it. What do we do with our children who cannot deal with it?" A couple of thoughts come to mind, *but let's move on.*

A doctor in Shaker Heights groused about the decision to run *Bonanza* instead of the New York Marathon, saying it was consistent with the view of Cleveland as a small town with pedestrian tastes. Finally, a TV fan in Clinton asked the station manager at Channel 8 to help him get an invitation to a state dinner at the White House. For some reason, the president wasn't answering his letters. When he didn't get the invitation, he turned to the FCC.

All the complainants got the same response. They were mailed a pamphlet explaining the FCC had no control over programming. Plus, pornography and obscenity had been narrowly defined by the courts. That probably didn't appease many, but most didn't write back.

The bottom line for the stations was always audience size.

What kind of news would increase ratings? Ron Bilek's opinion was this: "Viewers don't watch you if you give them a lot of news they should know about. You've got to give them a lot of news they want to know about and slip in the news they should know about." Av Westin, executive producer of ABC's *World News Tonight*, though differently. He said the most important stories ask these questions: "Is the world safe? Are my city and home safe? Are my loved ones safe?"

Ultimately, broadcasting is a business, and both management and talent have to do what's best for them. People in the industry move from station to station, often in the same city. You just have to remember where you are at any one time. Dawn Kendrick had been with WOIO for quite a while and took a job at WKYC. In one of her first live shots at Channel 3, she signed off with "19 Action News."

The anchors responded dryly, "Around here, we call it Channel 3 News."

"You should know better than to be here."

TV Reporters and Dangerous Locations

Tv NEWS CAN BE a tough job. Real tough. Dangerously tough. Just ask the videographers taping interviews with people who have talked themselves into a corner. Things can turn violent pretty quickly, and they go after the camera first to get rid of the evidence. But it can get pretty rough in other ways, and sometimes you have your life on the line.

It's not always intentional. In 1985, WKYC's Tom Sweeney was with a crew heading out to cover a story about the Ravenna Arsenal's conversion into an industrial park. They got to the intersection of Ohio 14 and Infirmary Road and came upon a car that had been hit by a tractor-trailer rig. The truck driver might not have realized that he had hit the car, and had kept on rolling. A woman who had seen the accident and who had just missed getting hit herself stopped to help the driver of the car on the side of the road. Sweeney got out to see what was happening—and suddenly another car skidded into them and sent Sweeney flying twenty feet. The woman who had stopped to help was knocked down; another car ran over her, then hit the disabled car. Sweeney ultimately recovered, but the good Samaritan, sadly, was killed.

Sometimes it's just a case of wrong place, wrong time. John Gerard found that out the hard way. When meteorologist Steve Browne left WKYC in July 1991, the station started looking at audition tapes to find a replacement. At that time, the station was owned by Multimedia Broadcasting, and Gerard came up from sister station WLWT-TV in Cincinnati to do weekend fill-ins. He made his debut on the Saturday six o'clock newscast, and at about 9:00 p.m. he ran back to the Sheraton City Centre Hotel around the corner on St. Clair. Gerard walked into a restroom and . . . crack! Someone hit him with a blackjack or club. Whatever it was, it did plenty of damage. He was supposed to do the eleven o'clock weather, but instead he was getting thirteen stitches in his head at Lutheran Medical Center. It was a robbery attempt. The guy who had jumped him kept demanding money, and Gerard even turned out his pockets to show he didn't have any. The assailant took off running.

Gerard went back to Cincinnati to recuperate. His wife said they held no grudge against Cleveland; the assault could have happened anywhere. But she added, "God was with him." (Oh, and as for remarks about the weatherman and "muggy" conditions, you can keep them; they were done to death at the time.)

A personal note from Mike Olszewski: Sometimes folks on the assignment desk don't use discretion when they send you out. In 1995, I was working weekends, and the annual Feast of the Assumption was being held in Little Italy. This was a tightly knit little neighborhood. At that time, if you didn't have black hair, or your first name didn't end with an "o" or "y," you probably didn't belong there. There had been an unfortunate incident a few years earlier when a school bus from an inner city neighborhood took a short cut down Mayfield Road and someone had thrown bricks at it.

The feast drew people from all over the city, and it was loud and colorful. All the stations could be expected to cover it. I was called to the desk, and they told me Tim Jenkins would be on camera. Tim was a really good camera guy, but there might be an issue, and we both knew it. Tim is black and we remembered what had happened to folks that didn't look like they belonged in Little Italy. We tried to explain, but all we heard was, "Just go." So we headed to Little Italy, knowing crowds would be drinking and we were going to stand out, especially Tim. He's well over six feet and stood head and shoulders over everyone else. We didn't mind covering the story, but we sure didn't want to *be* the story.

Well, if you've ever been to the feast, you know what parking is like. We found a spot but it was a hike to Mayfield Road. If we felt uncomfortable, we were just going to head back, but decided to see how the situation played out. When we made it to the crowd, a few dirty looks and comments started, but then something changed it immediately. Tim put the camera on his shoulder and everyone was our best friend! Every booth we visited handed us free food, so much we couldn't eat it, and plenty to bring back to the station. "You guys need a beer!" "Have you tried our cannoli?" "This is pizza like you've never had!" Everyone wanted screen time for their booth, and those egos might have helped us avoid a possible tense situation.

It wasn't always like that in Little Italy. Bob Cerminara could tell you that. He was with Channel 8 for a long time. Bob's a nice guy, but there's a certain intensity about him. He doesn't take any crap, but he's not going to give you any either. His reputation for being tough but fair gained the trust of a lot of elected officials who weren't as cooperative with other reporters.

Late one Saturday night there was a shooting on that stretch of Mayfield Road, and a young girl almost got hit. Police thought it was mob-related, and the assignment desk at Channel 8 made a point to call up Bob and videographer Ralph Tarsitano. Bob was curious: "Why us?" The desk said, "Because you're both Italian." Like that's going to matter. Bob said, "It doesn't matter if we're Greek or Polish or whatever. They're not going to talk to us!" At that point it was like arguing with a wall. You have the assignment, go.

Ethnic neighborhoods across the city are very tightly knit and protect their own. Bob and Ralph started interviewing and, as expected, weren't getting much. Then it got a little weird. No, a lot weird. They were at East 123rd and Mayfield when they noticed five or six guys running up to them. Their wives were behind them, crying, and the guys drew guns. Ralph nervously said, "I think we're in big trouble!" Bob tried to calm him down, but Ralph stressed, "You don't know this neighborhood like I do! This is not good!" These were some tough hombres and they had made it very clear they weren't happy. The guns were probably a pretty good indication.

"You know better than to come around here! What do you think you're doing?!"

Bob calmly explained why they were there, but it was like trying to reason with the assignment desk. Finally, one of them yelled out, "You're Italian, aren't you?!"

"Yeah. I'm Italian."

"Then you should know better than to be here."

Bob just said, "Yeah. We know better . . . but explain that to my boss!" There was a pause, and the guys started laughing. Time to pack up. They might not have parted friends, but they left on their feet.

Ralph Tarsitano can tell you another story about a very tough bird. Bill McKay had a well-established reputation as one of the best crime reporters anywhere. Even the old newspaper guys had the greatest respect for him, and Bill knew plenty of Cleveland's underworld on a first-name basis. That included a guy named Danny.

Let's get something clear right from the start. Danny Greene was not a nice man. If you were on his good side, you were fine— and you only wanted to be on his good side. The character in the film *Kill the Irishman* is not the same Danny Greene who worked the Cleveland rackets and took on the Mafia. One thing that was accurate was that Greene was not afraid to let his feelings known, and he could be very explicit. He also knew how to use the media.

In October 1977, the city had seen a series of car bombings that most reports linked to the war between Greene and the Mafia. It

"COME AND GET ME!" Mobster Danny Greene didn't like Italians and defied his enemies to track him down. Unfortunately for Greene, they took him up on his offer. *Cleveland Press Collection, Cleveland State University Archives*

was building to a boiling point, and Bill McKay was the obvious choice to track down Greene for an interview. They sent Ralph to do the camera. The pair tracked Greene down at his Celtic Club on North Waterloo Road. Greene didn't like Italians, but he put up with Ralph because he was with Bill McKay. This was clearly not a good day for Greene. When the two got to the club, they saw him waving a .45 in the air and screaming, "Hey you dagos! I'm here! Come and get me!" Seems there had been a package delivered to the club earlier that day addressed to Greene, a fish wrapped in paper. It wasn't a gift. It was a warning.

Ralph had been in tough situations before. If you're working with Bob Cerminara and Bill McKay, you sometimes ended up working in some pretty rough areas. Ralph remembered a shoot-out between mob families in the White City area. It was a concrete area down Lakeshore hill that didn't offer much protection from flying lead. The news people got out alive. The guys with the guns didn't.

Bill McKay convinced Greene to go on camera. They could have gone into the bar, but Greene didn't want an Italian in his Irish club. They did the interview in the street. Greene was a tall guy, a lot taller than Ralph. Ralph asked Greene to step over to the side of the street so he could stand on the curb for a better angle; otherwise, he would be looking up the Irishman's nose. Greene wasn't afraid of the bomb wars, and said flat out, "They'll never get me." He showed swagger, confidence, and bravado. And Greene ended the interview, saying he had a dentist appointment in Lyndhurst.

A few hours later he was killed in a car bombing at the Brainard Place office building, just after leaving his dentist's office.

And Then There Was Disco . . .

Weekday Fever

THE DISCO ERA STARTED in 1974, hit its peak with the John Travolta film *Saturday Night Fever* in 1977, and was taking its last raspy dying gasps in 1978.

Hey! What better time to start a daily afternoon disco dance show?

That's when WKYC started *Weekday Fever*, advertised as the nation's first (and very likely only) locally produced disco show. It ran Monday through Friday at 4:00 p.m., a time of day when everyone felt like dressing up in white suits, black shirts and neck chains and dancing around the house, right? Right. These were the days of two-income households; who was supposed to watch this show—latchkey kids?

Granted, the show had two solid hosts. Tim Byrd was the most popular disc jockey at WGCL-FM, which had a big teenage audience with its Top 40 format (though Top 40 didn't include a whole lot of disco). Nancy Glass was from Boston. She had co-hosted a short-lived morning talk show on WKYC that had tried to compete with *The Morning Exchange*. The two auditioned with a pack of other hopefuls and got the nod from an audience research survey of teenagers and women eighteen to forty-nine. (Eighteen to forty-nine? As if you would see a teenager dancing with a woman pushing fifty at a local club, but hey—it was their show.) John Pike, then the program director at Channel 3, said that was the audience they were after because they were "the people who buy products in America." Right. Like chewing gum and diapers. Let's see where this leads.

Ratings for Channel 3 at that time of day were stagnant. The

THE BYRD LANDS AT NITE MOVES: Disc jockey Tim Byrd hoped his audience at WGCL-FM would follow him to the afternoon disco show he hosted on WKYC. The TV ratings soon showed they didn't. *Cleveland Press Collection, Cleveland State University Archives*

station was getting beaten by the *Merv Griffin Show* and *Brady Bunch* reruns. These were important hours leading up to the evening news block, where Channel 3 needed some help. To add some flash to the new production, they selected for the show's location a trendy venue nearby on Playhouse Square.

Entrepreneurs Bob Hammer and Barry Weingart had taken over the old Alpine Village nightclub and transformed it into a dance club called Nite Moves. Weingart had been around the local scene for some time, even working early FM rock radio with Steve Nemeth, who was better known as Doc Nemo. The club had multiple floors overlooking a huge dance floor, and that looked like a winner to the show's producers.

To John Pike's credit, he did admit to being the last person you would expect to produce a show of this type. He told the *Cleveland Press*, "I'm so inhibited that I've got to be twenty-seven sheets to the wind to get up and dance." Regardless, he was now charged

KICK UP YOUR HEELS: Tim Byrd and co-host Nancy Glass would both go on to long and successful TV careers. It's unlikely that WKYC's *Weekday Fever* showed up on either of their resumes. *Cleveland Press Collection, Cleveland State University Archives*

with assembling a team that would get the midday audience up disco dancing and pointing their fingers in the air.

If you have a dance show, you need dancers. The producers held auditions, and as many as 80 volunteers would show up every Saturday, with five changes of clothing, to tape the next week's shows. Channel 3 had mobile trucks set up like a command post in back of the club, and only had a few hours to get five shows in the can before the club's regular crowd started showing up. It was pretty much live-to-tape. Then the show's dancers went home to shower and, one would assume, head out dancing for the night.

Weekday Fever wasn't all bobbing around on the dance floor. There would be dance tips, maybe a guest star, and Nancy's fashion and gossip segments. Granted, some of the gossip was pretty weak. ("Donna Summer's new record will be shaped like a heart!" Call the neighbors! Wake the kids!) This was a chance for Nancy to get out on the road to do features on "disco life"—which could turn really strange really quick. One segment had her standing in line outside New York's Studio 54, which was by that point pretty much a tourist trap. Its best days were behind it, but people still tried to get in just to say they had been there. In one segment, Nancy was interviewing people in line and came across a transvestite who said he was a law student. To Nancy's credit, she was able to do the interview with a straight face, at least in front of the camera.

There were other bizarre segments. Now and then Nancy would highlight certain dance partners, including two who were brother and sister. As she told *The Plain Dealer*, "That was interesting by itself . . . until you learned that they have been teaching senior citizens how to disco—that's special." And just a thought . . . maybe a little dangerous.

Tim Byrd had a lot of faith in the show. In fact, he quit his midday gig at WGCL-FM to concentrate on *Weekday Fever* and personal appearances at some of the local dance halls. Plus, he was still able to use his radio instinct for his "Pick of the Week" tunes. (In truth, WGCL was in a constant state of turmoil from the top down. Many would say you didn't quit the company that owned it. You escaped.) Tim knew a hit, and thanks to him, *Weekday Fever* tagged seven songs that were million-sellers. The show even received some gold records. Chic's "Le Freak" and Donna Summer's take on "MacArthur Park" got their first airing on *Fever*. Groups like the Village People and Trammps stopped by, and work continued to keep everyone's feet moving.

During that time, the syndicated *SCTV* aired late, and one of its recurring skits might have been an omen for the future of *Weekday*

Fever. "Mel's Rock Pile" was a parody of a disco dance show that came really close to what was seen on Channel 3 every day. Kids dancing, the host in a white suit dancing stiffly, and strange interviews and lifestyle pieces. The *SCTV* crew had taped a special in Cleveland that same year. Inspiration? You decide.

By the time Tim had quit his radio gig in early 1979, *Fever* was already on the ropes. Program director John Like admitted that ratings never reached the station's expectations, although it did reach as high as number two. He said the station had no plans to cancel *Fever*, but the writing was on the wall. Eventually the station cured itself of *Weekday Fever*, and it was back to reruns.

There were other dance shows. Nina Blackwood was a former Clevelander and one of the original MTV "veejays." In 1990, she hosted *Electric Avenue* from Club Coconuts in the Flats on WJW. It was only on once a week, and it wasn't long before that got short-circuited, too.

Even so, the *Fever* hosts ended up in better places. Both Tim and Nancy went on to bigger careers. Tim would become one of the original VH-1 "veejays" and Nancy would be seen all over syndicated TV, including *Inside Edition* and *American Journal*. Gotta wonder if *Weekday Fever* is on either of their résumés.

"Pretty and Perky and Straight of Proboscis"

Cleveland's First Female News Anchor Arrives

IT'S NOT EASY TO be the first of anything. People judge you differently, and you're always the center of attention. You live your life under a microscope. Just ask Amanda Arnold, Cleveland's first female news anchor.

Amanda grew up in Houston, but was a noon anchor in Baltimore when she beat two hundred others who auditioned for the gig at Cleveland's Channel 3 with Doug Adair. That was in 1978. She didn't know there was that much competition for the job until she read about it in the local ads and trade papers. WKYC did a huge media campaign welcoming its new anchor, and even set up a news conference to introduce her. This was going to be a very big deal. Channel 3 and NBC executives were on hand to welcome Amanda to Cleveland. Turns out, Amanda almost never got to Cleveland, and she's still amazed that she's alive to talk about it today.

Here's the way Amanda remembers it: "Around dusk the evening before, soon after the movers had gotten underway after finally emptying my townhouse in Baltimore, I was making my way solo through a slushy rain and snowstorm on the 308-mile drive to Cleveland via the Pennsylvania Turnpike. Suddenly I had no functioning windshield wipers or defroster!" A fuse in her Volvo had shorted out. Amanda didn't even know cars needed fuses, so she didn't have any extras . . . but that wouldn't have helped much anyway.

She continues: "I couldn't even see well enough to safely exit the turnpike and, of course, this being long before the days of cell phones, I had no way to call and say, 'Hey, got some troubles here! Can you postpone the event?'" There were some very important people waiting in Cleveland, and failure wasn't an option.

Her car was full of stuff she would need before the movers arrived, the press and network brass were standing by to welcome her, and, as Amanda puts it, she had "a morning deadline where my TV bosses and the media would be expecting their new anchor-woman to rise to the occasion. I knew I had no choice but to keep going."

Do you remember the winters back then? They're pretty hard to forget, and this storm was typical. Big clumps of wet snow, driving rain and slush, and no defroster in the car. Little if any visibility, but Amanda soldiered on. The only part of the windshield that was clear was a one-inch square in the corner. You make do with what you have!

"I kept hunched over to peer through that tiny space the size of a postage stamp, and occasionally gave my neck and back a rest by sitting up straight and following the blurry red taillights of slow-moving trucks weaving in and out ahead of me.

"Hours later, on grace and a prayer, I managed to make it into Cleveland with one hour to spare. I freshened up at the hotel, changed clothes, spruced the hair and makeup, then sailed on in, cool and calm, to meet and greet the execs and media at 9:00 a.m., right on time."

Amanda's Cleveland adventure had begun, but the main event was yet to come. Her debut was going to make Cleveland TV history. No pressure there, right? There had been a huge promotional push leading up to the "rollout." Amanda had made it through a horrible storm, met the media and the next stop was the news desk, right? Not so much.

"It was two days before my highly touted news debut. WKYC had aired a torrent of promotional TV spots where I was seen walking briskly along some outdoor street while saying to the camera, 'I don't *feel* like a star, and I hope I don't *act* like one . . . I like . . . covering real stories about real people, folks who care about the

AMANDA ARNOLD'S CLEVELAND ADVENTURE: Local TV's first female news anchor battled winter storms and a slippery floor during her time at WKYC. *Cleveland Press Collection, Cleveland State University Archives*

news as much as I do—*and* bananas on my chocolate ice cream!' For some reason, that line really caught on. I heard it echoed by countless viewers throughout my two years in Cleveland.

"The station had placed full-page ads in *The Plain Dealer*: A smiling close-up of my face, bigger than life itself, with the bold caption: 'Amanda Arnold: somebody you just know you're going to like.'" As a result of that press conference and other interviews, print reporters also had written several favorable and anticipatory feature articles.

Finally, the big night arrived, though Amanda says it was almost anti-climactic because it went well.

She hadn't been sure how Doug Adair would react to her, she

A PAIR WITH DOUG ADAIR: Amanda Arnold's fears that her long-established co-anchor might not welcome her were quickly diminished. *Cleveland Public Library*

said, but "We worked well together. We liked and respected each other, and the viewers knew that, too. While always remaining professional during the news portions of the broadcast, sometimes, before tossing to commercials and between the weather and sports segments, Doug and I would fence back and forth with some good-natured banter. Oh, Doug could be a sly one, sometimes teasing and testing me a bit on-the-air, but he was fun to work with, and we kept each other on our toes."

Amanda settled in for a long stay. Then, disaster.

About a month after the debut, she said, "I fell in my bathroom and broke my nose!"

It wasn't merely a broken nose. On a Sunday morning Amanda slipped in the bathroom of her Shaker Square apartment, went face first into the tile, and the impact drove her teeth into her lip. Plus, it knocked her out cold. The next thing she remembered was the building superintendent trying to locate a doctor. But, oddly enough, in the late 1970s, that was no easy job because doctors enjoyed weekends off, too.

As the *Press*' Bill Barrett described the accident and the follow-up, it was "the most important nose job to date in Northeast Ohio." He called Amanda for an update and she said she wanted to be back on the six and eleven o'clock newscasts within a week, "pretty and perky and straight of proboscis." At that point he just had a hard time understanding her. "Ride now I loog like a chipmug. I'b sorry. No pictures."

Cleveland has world-class medical care, and Amanda saw it first-hand when she was eventually taken to the emergency room. They put a cast on her nose, and that, along with the green bruises around her eyes, just wouldn't put her in the best light. But that wasn't the end of it. She tried cold compresses, but the swelling wasn't going down. She said, "My nose was starting to look funny, out of line. So I called Chuck Gerber, our station manager at Channel 3." He was able to locate a plastic surgeon who could do some alignment work. A few days later, the cast came off.

The public had to wait. It might have worked in her favor. Amanda says, "That, of course, generated even more buzz . . . maybe actually in a weird way, it caused me to be even more swiftly accepted and embraced by the viewers, as I surely was. Immediately, I started getting empathetic letters, and generous coverage by *The Plain Dealer*'s Bill Hickey, providing me comfort, consolation, and encouragement. 'After all,' many wrote in effect, 'our own Ohioan and American hero John Glenn had fallen in *his* bathroom, so you're in good company. Welcome to Cleveland!'" What a welcome!

A Fine Line Between
Serious and Silly

Sports and Weather

SPORTS AND WEATHER TOGETHER, the one-two punch in the second half of the show that stations bet will keep you tuned in to the whole newscast. In recent years weather has crept up to the first half of most newscasts, pretty much teasing the in-depth forecast at the tail end of the show. If the sports teams are hot, they figure you'll want details. Stations put a lot of thought and research into how they present the news. But when the red light goes on, it still comes down to the person looking into the lens. Every station wants the next Al Roker or Dan Patrick. No pressure there, right?

First, let's get a look at the guys working the weather maps. Years ago that part of the newscast was pretty straightforward. Is it going to be sunny? Rainy? What's the high tomorrow? In the early days, Ron Penfound at Channel 5 was known to do sports, weather, and even news. Before that, Joe Finan was the "Atlantic weather man," and he dressed up like a service station attendant. By the seventies, *The Plain Dealer*'s TV critic said, "One station had a straight man at the map, another featured a comedian, and the third put on some bubblehead beauty queen." To be fair, even network guys fell into those categories. NBC's Willard Scott paid a visit to Cleveland and said flat out, "I'm not a meteorologist. I'm a performer." If you wanted people to tune in night after night, you had to be totally original and leave them wanting more.

Joe Conway replaced Al Roker at WKYC in 1983. He suggested you had to walk a fine line between serious and silly. As he told Maria Riccardi, "You don't want to be a clown, and you don't want to be a bore. You want to fall somewhere in between."

There's a lot riding on the weather segment, and sometimes people will switch in the middle of a newscast to get the best of all worlds. Some research showed weather to be the biggest draw after the news anchors.

According to *The Plain Dealer*, Conway was not going to rest until he had found something to set him apart from the other "weatherblabbers" in town. One night he introduced "biometeorology." Wha? He explained it as a scientific method for predicting your mood based on the weather. A mood forecast! As *The Plain Dealer* saw it, "Now you can rely on Conway's multi-colored 'Weather Health Index' to tell you if your boss is going to yell at you, how much Bufferin you'll need, and what kind of precautions you should take before stepping in front of a bus."

Conway's weekend weather counterpart at Channel 3 was Paul Edmunds. The pair were tagged by *The Plain Dealer* as "radar rodents" who did their segments like *Circus of the Stars* . . . without any stars. Paul once did his weather report from the Channel 3 Christmas party. The segments actually seemed pretty pointless. In a segment that ran way too long, he ran out of things to say to Del Donahoo and ended by thanking Del's wife for the great coffee she made for the morning team.

Another time Paul did his segment outside Cleveland Municipal Stadium where Michael Jackson and his family would be staging their "Victory Tour" that evening. You guessed it. There's Paul in a red leather jacket, sunglasses . . . and that bit fell flat real quickly.

At WJW, Dick Goddard seemed to evolve over the years along with the importance of the weather person. With more than fifty years in the business, he has seen plenty of changes. One was "the hook"—something that you identified with as well as the audience. Dick hit the mother lode with his love for animals, and of all things, a caterpillar.

Legend had it the stripes on the woolly bear caterpillar could predict the severity of the upcoming winter. Dick championed the forecasting woolly bear, and eventually the annual Woolly Bear

Festival in Vermilion began to draw crowds of 100,000 and more.

Despite that, *The Plain Dealer* said, "Goddard's dignified approach would be of interest to a funeral director." He had some odd habits, too. He said his perfect evening was "sitting outside on the porch . . . watching lightning." Maybe he didn't have cable.

Let's talk a bit about Dick and the animals. You can meet Dick on the street and tell him you're crippled by shingles and the conversation will somehow be directed to cocker spaniels or some other breed. Here's a story that has been told before, but it's a classic. (We also encourage you to read his book, *Six Inches of Partly Cloudy*, for similar tales.)

Former Congressman Dennis Kucinich was walking down the aisle for a third time in August 2005. This time around it was to very attractive Englishwoman, Elizabeth Harper (who, coincidentally, lived near Cleveland Street in her hometown). Over the years Dennis had become friends with quite a few celebrities, and he invited several to the wedding at Cleveland City Hall. Why he would choose that location, considering his one stormy term at city hall, is anyone's guess, but hey . . . it was his wedding! Dennis also invited lots of Cleveland friends, including plenty from the media. For a time starting back in 1990, Dennis was a political analyst at TV-8. Sure enough, Dick Goddard was on the list.

Tim Taylor tells it in *Six Inches of Partly Cloudy*, but others have told the same tale. It was an outdoor wedding on the mall, and Dick got a seat next to . . . get this . . . Sean Penn. The same Sean Penn who doesn't always want to see a camera lens pointed at him, and there are plenty of paparazzi with black eyes who will tell you that. They just didn't tell Dick.

He asked Sean if he could get a picture, and . . . snap . . . there was a photo. All eyes were on Dick and Sean. Sean said in a firm but friendly tone, "I'm a guest here, as you are. I would hope you would respect my anonymity here." Dick was very apologetic and extended an olive branch in true Goddard fashion. He invited Sean to the Woollybear Festival.

Then there was Shirley MacLaine.

The ceremony ended and there was an hour wait to the reception so Dennis and the missus could have photos taken. Everyone went to the hotel bar on the next street before heading back to the City Hall rotunda for food and more drinks. Who walked in but Shirley MacLaine, with a dog on a leash. Most people were looking at Shirley, who sat down next to Sean Penn. Dick was looking at the dog. Most people respected MacLaine's and Penn's privacy, but step aside—Dick Goddard had to say hello to Fido. Everybody was watching what happened next.

As Dick started getting acquainted with Shirley's canine friend, she didn't hold back: "Please don't pet him; he's very leery of people, and he's sleeping." She didn't know Dick Goddard from Adam, of course, and, chances are she really didn't care.

Dick tried to get on Shirley's good side by saying, "You know, Shirley, while you were in movies, I was starring in *Damn Yankees* at Kent State." Then he started singing "You Gotta Have Heart." She didn't give a damn about that, either. Everyone who knew Dick was just sitting back and enjoying the show. For the moment, Dick looked as if he realized what was happening and backed off.

But then, Dick got it into his head that he needed a picture with Shirley's dog. "No" was not an option. Shirley was minding her own business when she looked down and there was Dick on his hands and knees while his buddy snapped away. That worked at Shirley's last nerve, and she exploded, "Get the [bleep] off my dog!"

Joe Conway didn't have dogs or caterpillars for a "hook," but he did have his computerized weather bunny, "Ralph the Rabbit." Alas, the public wasn't clamoring for any Ralph Festivals.

Dan Dobrowolski at WEWS was known for his zucchini recipes. That's right, zucchini. But let's face it, how many zucchini recipes are there, and who really cares? When he was profiled in *The Plain Dealer* in early 1985, his agent was passing around audition tapes to other markets. Dan said his appeal was that he was "just like anybody else, the regular guy. Maybe just a little more demented."

What do you do if your competition is your wife? That happened on occasion with Andre and Sally Bernier. Sally graduated from

NO PHOTOS! Both actress Shirley MacLaine and fellow actor Sean Penn told Dick Goddard to put away his camera at Dennis Kucinich's wedding.

West Geauga High School and met Andre at Lyndon State College in Vermont. They worked together for a time, got married, and started traveling the country. Andre landed a gig in Cedar Rapids, and after just a few months, got an offer at the Weather Channel. They hired Sally as well, but the couple didn't work together on-air until they moved to a station in Minneapolis. It wasn't long before "the weather couple" was a staple of the morning show, usually with Sally on set and Andre braving the elements in a split screen. Sally obviously got the better of that deal. Then, they moved on to Cleveland.

Andre landed at Channel 8, Sally at Channel 43. Now and then Andre would fill in for Dick Goddard on the eleven o'clock newscast, and Sally was on a few minutes before with the *Ten O'Clock News*. The folks at home could compare forecasts, which could be different, and it made for some interesting dinner talk when the Berniers were back home.

*   *   *

And now, Sports . . .

In the 1980s, when the Browns were hot, sportscasters reigned supreme. Before the days of ESPN, sports talk radio, and twenty-four-hour coverage, TV sportscasters were the best way to find out what everyone else would be talking about the next day. As with weather, facts are facts; there's only so much information and so many ways to present it. So personality was the key, especially on a slow news day.

Stations were always looking for a new way to put sports in front of the public. Before WOIO had a news department, the station had radio's Bruce Drennan host a panel discussion show called *Let's Talk Sports* with newspaper writers from around the state. Content was important but it wasn't everything. There was also the likability factor. As one TV executive put it, "If your anchor was Jesus Christ, it would take Cleveland two to three years to see if it could stand him." It also helped to be a fan of Cleveland sports. If fans thought you were one of them, you were gold. If you crossed the line, you weren't going to be around long.

Remember Wayland Boot? If you do, you have a good memory. He came to Channel 3 from KOIN in Portland in 1984. He was known as Ed Wayland in the Northwest, and he got a lot of positive press when he set up shop at WKYC. He said, "Sports is more show business than journalism. I give 'em the pertinent stuff first, but it's mostly entertainment. If I'm doing something like Michael Ray Richardson kicking his drug habit, that's news. But if Cleveland loses to or beats Buffalo, that's entertainment." Wayland wanted to do sports for people who don't like sports. He could be pretty glib in his comments, too. Wayland once said the Cavs "looked better than Lola Falana" in the first half of a game, and "worse than Don King's hair" in the second.

He had a bag of on-air tricks, too. Once commenting on a play he said, "Even Stymie couldn't believe it!" and cut to a clip of Stymie Beard from the Little Rascals blinking his eyes. The Burnt Biscuit award for sports bloopers showed a baby gnawing on—what else?—a biscuit. Then, "a little traveling music"—with blues music as a bed over the out-of-town scores. He was entertaining, but *The Plain Dealer*'s James Ewinger went so far as to say part of Wayland's success was because he presented a "non-threatening black image. He comes dangerously close to the jokin', happy, not-quite-shufflin' sort of figure who knows how to have a good time." Keep in mind that was James Ewinger's opinion . . . and Wayland certainly didn't agree with it!

He did agree that the Browns teams of the 1950s and 1960s were in a class of their own—and his insurance agent was Lou "The Toe" Groza.

Then one day the roof caved in for Wayland. A reporter from Oregon called to do a "Where Are They Now?" type report. When he asked how Wayland was adjusting to life in Cleveland, Wayland replied, "Comparing Cleveland and Portland is like comparing a Ferrari and a dump truck." Uh-oh. Instant uproar!

Wayland apologized on the air. Twice! Later he tried to explain it by saying he didn't mean to insult anyone. He said, "The Ferrari being, it's just a faster pace in the Pacific Northwest. 'Dump truck' just being a 'roll up your sleeves, go to work' mentality." Nobody bought that line, and the talk shows were on it like piranhas. When his contract came up in January 1987, Wayland was heading back to Ferrari-ville. Back to being Ed Wayland, though he continued playing the Stymie Beard clips when he returned to KOIN.

The famous big top owner P.T. Barnum is given credit for saying, "There's no such thing as bad publicity." Granted, TV news might be likened to a circus, but even Barnum would have had a hard time with some of the headlines from local newsrooms.

Jim Mueller was a familiar face on WJKW. He'd been with the station since 1974, but by the early 1980s his relationship with management had become strained. Mueller was in contract talks, and they eventually reached a boiling point. In March of 1981, Mueller took it to a different level. He filed a million-dollar libel suit in Cuyahoga County Common Pleas Court against Storer Broadcasting, news director Virgil Dominic, and general manager Bill Flynn.

In the suit, Mueller claimed his reputation had been damaged by a series of memos. The *Cleveland Press* ran down the charges that Mueller said had falsely described him as "dishonest, unmotivated, lazy, irresponsible, incompetent as a broadcaster, and unwilling to learn new techniques." The suit claimed Mueller would "suffer financial hardship, loss of time, mental anguish, and emotional distress in his efforts to refute the unfounded charges." It also described the working conditions as intolerable. One of the management memos reportedly said that a previous evening's sports report "looked old and tired." It also stated Mueller had been denied an assignment because management wasn't convinced he could cover it with "creativity and imagination."

Perhaps the most damning claims came in a statement attributed to Dominic that said, "Your attitude and job performance continue to increase my doubts as to whether you are suitable for the program and staff requirements at TV-8." Mueller's attorney, Robert J. Rotatori, was quoted in *The Plain Dealer* saying the company and its management "deliberately set on a course of action to destroy his reputation in the broadcasting community."

It wasn't likely the contract negotiations would be any easier!

Just a few hours after the lawsuit was filed, Mueller, working without a contract, did the sports on the six o'clock show. He was suspended a short time later.

The folks at Channel 8 denied the charges.

There's an old saying: "The color of truth is gray." Dominic told the *Press* he was "dumbfounded" by the charges. He said, "We thought we had made it clear we would like him to continue here with us. We made him a contact offer—his agent turned it down." Mueller was represented by super-agent Ed Keating, who had handled some of the biggest names in local broadcasting. There were rumors WKYC was already talking to him about bringing Mueller over to Channel 3.

While the courts sorted out the details, Mueller took a job as vice-president in charge of public relations with a local construction company. It was likely a part-time gig until the dust settled over the lawsuit, but there was also speculation the writing was on the wall. Channels 3 and 5 were quoted in a newspaper report saying as many as ten staffers at WJKW had approached them about jumping ship.

TV people are like nomads, and they expect to work at a number of stations in their careers. But ten staffers leaving at one time was really out of the ordinary. Again, dissatisfaction with Flynn and Dominic was said to be the issue. Let's look at all sides here. Emotions can run high when you think your job is at stake, and there was a rumor Storer Broadcasting was thinking of dumping its terrestrial stations to concentrate on cable.

Broadcast people will often quote the unwritten rule that lawsuits can get you blackballed when you apply for another job. Who wants to hire someone who's not afraid to take you to court? That wasn't the case with Mueller. He moved on to Channel 3, replacing Joe Pellegrino in 1982, and he continued to call the Browns games on radio at WWWE. After a few years, he went on to become a familiar voice for one of Northeast Ohio's most successful car dealers. WJKW seemed to do all right as well.

TV news viewers are creatures of habit. They have their favorites and can have a hard time accepting change. Nev Chandler became a favorite of the Cleveland sports audience until his death in 1994. But after he took over for Gib Shanley, one of the legends of Cleveland broadcasting, at WEWS in 1985, viewers needed time to adjust. For years, people would call Nev "Gib," and he'd get mail addressed to "Nev Shanley" or "Gib Chandler."

Nev would often imitate other sports people, such as Herb Score, but that was off the air. A native Clevelander, he had always wanted to be a sportscaster. His aunt Betty Nickel had worked on radio, and when he was a kid, she arranged to have Nev sit in the broadcast booth during an Indians game with Bob Neal and Jimmy Dudley. It was well known that the two men loathed each other (see volume I of *Cleveland TV Tales* for their story); hopefully, they watched their language around their guest for the day.

Nev was briefly on the doomed WKBF news, from late 1968

. . . BUT NOT FORGOTTEN: WEWS sports anchor Nev Chandler was one of Northeast Ohio's most popular TV personalities when cancer claimed him at the age of just 48.
Cleveland Press Collection, Cleveland State University Archives

until the news department shut down in November 1970. He used that time to let Cleveland get to know him. It worked, too. He landed a gig at WEWS, where he got to work with Shanley, one of his idols. It was a time when sportscasters were getting a lot more attention. Nev remembered a meeting he had had with Gib and the station's general manager, Ed Cervenak: "I'll never forget it. He called Shanley and me into his office and said he wanted a commentary every day. Gib said, 'What if there's nothing to opinionate about?' Cervenak said he didn't care. People talk about sports all the time and he wanted an opinion every day." Keep in mind you had maybe three and a half minutes, tops, to get out all the scores, breaking stories, and the occasional editorial, so you had to use your words prudently.

About the breaking stories—handling them can be like a chess game.

Chandler gained a feather in his cap when he broke the story that one of the Browns' most popular players, Bob Golic, was heading to L.A. to sign with the Raiders as a free agent. He already had an interview with Golic in the can, but sat on the story for the six o'clock report. He later said, "We took a chance that nobody else knew about Golic leaving, and saved it for eleven." Stations constantly monitor each other, and there would have been a feeding frenzy to get the story on later that night. The other stations wouldn't be able to get Golic after eleven, and he boarded a plane early the next day. Score one for Team Chandler!

Other sports guys got the big stories, too, but sometimes it generated some nervous moments. Casey Coleman saw that first hand. Casey started in radio but jumped to WJW-TV within just a few years, in 1982. He resembled his dad, the legendary Ken Coleman, but he had the chops, too. And he wasn't afraid to point fingers and name names, which even he admitted "might have put some people off."

Casey had spent a good part of his childhood in Cleveland before moving away when his father, Ken Coleman, took the play-by-play job with the Boston Red Sox in 1965. When Casey came back, he thought local media handled sports figures with "kid gloves." Later, when Art Modell moved the Browns to Baltimore, Casey was accused of giving Modell same kid-glove treatment. Modell and the Colemans had been friends since Casey was a kid, so he scored a coup when he landed an interview. But the switchboards lit up from angry viewers when Casey opened the interview saying the decision had to be tough for Modell. Now, that really is a big story.

Casey was pretty well connected with the sports world and national media. On June 27, 1986, a source at CNN told him that Browns safety Don Rogers had just died of a cocaine overdose. Casey jumped on the phone with the hospital, and a nurse con-

K.C. BECOMES CASEY: The son of famed sportscaster Ken Coleman, Ken Jr., used his initials as his stage name when he, too, came to Cleveland's airwaves. *Cleveland Press Collection, Cleveland State University Archives*

fided that, yes, Rogers was dead. This is a story that should have exploded on the wire services, but there had been no official coroner's report. Casey decided to take a chance and break the story at eleven. It was a long night for him after that because no one else, including CNN, was reporting Rogers' death. Then the radio talk shows chimed in—and took aim at Casey, criticizing him because he was the only one reporting the cocaine overdose. He was vindicated later in the day when the story was confirmed, but those were very nervous hours for Mr. Coleman!

Casey Coleman came from local TV royalty. His father, Ken, had been the voice of Cleveland sports at WEWS and had called games for the Browns and Indians. But Casey's first choice was a career in law. "Dad always wanted me to be a sportscaster," he said. "But I grew up in the 1960s, and it was fashionable then to do something different than what your parents wanted." Not only that, he knew well that the long hours of a sportscaster's job kept him away from the family. "I grew up with my dad doing the six and eleven o'clock news with Tom Field, Dorothy Fuldheim and Joe Finan, and we barely saw him." But Casey's dad also had given him some savvy advice. When Casey started thinking seriously about broadcasting, Ken told him the most important thing was to learn how to ad lib. Casey eventually returned to radio, and passed away in 2006, ad-libbing right to the end.

Dads can be a big influence in sports—and in sports broadcasting. Jim Donovan at WKYC once said, "My father was everything to me—father, coach, friend, and adviser. When I was a boy he took me to all the Boston Bruins (hockey) games. I'd take a recorder with me. That's when I first started announcing games. When I was working in places like St. Cloud, Minnesota, years ago, homesick, and not making much money, he would tell me to hang in there."

Gib Shanley told the same story.

Gib grew up in Bellaire, Ohio. When he started to think about a career in radio, his dad said he needed the right training and sent him to a broadcasting school in Washington, D.C. Shanley worked in a couple of small markets after that and then earned a shot at the big-time in 1961 doing sports at WGAR in Cleveland. From there he went on to WEWS for eighteen years, had a brief try at the Los Angeles media market, and then came back to Cleveland at WUAB in January 1988.

Gib was still a huge name in Cleveland, and the only real name on the WUAB news staff when it first went on the air. He said, "People would ask me why I was at a minor-league station." That question didn't sit well with him. Gib pointed out that in the late 1980s, WUAB was picked up on cable stations all over Ohio because it wasn't a network affiliate.

By the time he joined WUAB, Gib was introducing stories from sports reporters Jeff Phelps and Ron Jantz, and that suited him just fine. He said he didn't want to sit on camera too long and bore people. He saw plenty of changes, too. "There's more entertainment now and not enough substance," he said.

Let's face it. The sports anchors often had a tough job generating excitement about Cleveland's pro teams. But high school football was a draw, and it paid off well for Channel 8. Dan Coughlin and Tony Rizzo would fly in the WJW news copter to games all over Northeast Ohio, and the crowds loved it, too. They covered all of Northeast Ohio. Dan is one of the great storytellers in Northeast Ohio, and tells about "Friday Night Lights" in his own book *Pass the Nuts*, which is terrific. He says, "Rizzo said it made him feel like a rock star! We'd fly in, stay a quarter, and move on to the next game." That is, if the helicopter cooperated.

One Friday night, Dan and videographer Doug Herrmann were heading back from Norwalk and decided to fit in one more game. Olmsted Falls was on the way; they could tape a few plays and run back to the station. They would usually call ahead and let police know they were stopping by a particular field, and the cops would be there with flares to show them where to land.

As they were heading toward Olmsted Falls, a light flashed on in the cockpit. They were able to land in back of the stadium, and the crew ran out to get footage, then came back—and saw their pilot on top of the copter wielding wrench. This did not look good. "We're not flying back tonight." This was a job for a repair crew from the airport, and that wasn't happening until at least the next day. Dan and Doug grabbed a cab back to the station and barely made it in time for their news show.

Despite occasional bumpy rides, Dan says the copter spoiled him: "You're flying out to a game in Massillon and you come over the bluff. There it is . . . Paul Brown Stadium! You land behind the scoreboard, and the fans love it. They sure appreciated the attention."

Then there were sights most folks don't get to see. The copter was based at Burke Lakefront Airport, but if you were cleared to fly near Hopkins, the sight of all the runway lights crisscrossing the field was something that stayed with you.

We mentioned you had to clear it with police before you landed, Well, one time somebody forgot that detail, and when the Channel 8 copter landed at Willoughby South High School unannounced, the cops made their displeasure clear—with guns drawn!

Helicopters need a pretty wide area to land safely, and can still cause problems after they do. "One night," Dan recalls, "we were heading out to cover the Akron Hoban game against Walsh Jesuit. They told us to land at the baseball field, but that was after a really dry fall season. We set it down right on top of the pitcher's mound. It kicked up so much dust, they had to delay the game until it settled!"

Then there was the guy watching through the fence at the side of the field. Someone said he might have coached another sport. Dan saw "he had this wild look in his eye. We heard he told people he had been a killer in Vietnam and claimed he was a master with a knife!" As Dan and the crew passed by, the guy muttered, "This reminds me of 'Nam!" They got out of there as soon as possible.

"This is Dan Rather. Who Am I Speaking To?"

THE REAL TEST OF a newsroom comes with breaking stories, and stories don't come any bigger than the events of March 30, 1981. Ronald Reagan was shot by John Hinckley, Jr. outside the Washington Hilton as the president was walking to his limo after a speech. In situations like that, stations go to network coverage, but will want a local angle for their own evening news show. Sometimes it comes wrapped in a bow.

Reagan had only been in office a few months and, as with all U.S. Presidents, was followed by cameras everywhere. The attempt on his life was on the air in minutes, and newsrooms everywhere scrambled for a new angle. Rick DeChant was working the assignment desk at WJKW when a call came to Dick Goddard. Dick yelled out, "I think you should take this call." It was an elderly woman who had asked to speak to Dick because he was her favorite part of the news, but what she had to offer had nothing to do with the weather. She told DeChant that she'd seen the video of the shooting several times and was pretty sure the guy in the yellow sweater who had jumped on Hinckley was her neighbor in Garfield Heights!

This isn't something you rush on air. It's important to get a story first, and far more important to get it right. Rick DeChant got the woman's address and pulled out one of those old crisscross directories that showed names, phone numbers and addresses by street. There was the name she had given him: Al Antenucci in Garfield Heights! DeChant called the house, and a man answered. "Who am I speaking to?" DeChant asked. "I'm an agent with the Secret Service," was the answer. It was a major break in the story.

It turned out that Al Antenucci, the president of Cleveland Carpenters Union Local 1750, was in Washington for a conference. When he heard that Reagan would be speaking nearby, he walked over to the Hilton thinking maybe he could get a glimpse—and ended up getting a lot more. Antenucci was right next Hinckley, and jumped on him right after the shooting.

The folks at Channel 8 kept their cards close to the vest. A news crew raced out to Garfield Heights to interview Mrs. Antenucci. They got her reaction and some b-roll of family photos, and the local story gained a new lead. Rick checked out the video and called CBS to share the story. He gave some details to a producer, who said, "Hang on. Someone wants to speak to you."

The next voice said, "This is Dan Rather. Who am I speaking to?" Gulp! Rick explained the details and promised to put the story "on the bird" (the satellite feed.) WJKW had the story on first, but it led the network news right afterward.

About a week later, news director Virgil Dominic posted a note on the newsroom bulletin board. It was from a scratch pad that read: "From the Desk of Dan Rather." The handwritten note congratulated Dan's "colleagues" at Channel 8 and called the Antenucci story a great effort. It went on to say how CBS was so grateful for the great work done by its affiliates, and this report was a prime example.

It's times like that that make you think it's all worth it.

"Do You Own The City?"

Carl Stokes Begins His TV Career

1967 WAS A HUGE YEAR in Cleveland's history—and the nation's. That's because Carl Stokes had broken a racial barrier to become the first African American elected mayor of a major U.S. city. All eyes were now on Cleveland, and there was plenty of pressure on Stokes to see whether he would be successful. TV had only been around twenty years, but by now it had already become the primary news medium.

Stokes was a young, handsome, charismatic guy, so getting his message out via television was a logical step. But some questioned his logic when he accepted his first weekly TV series.

WKBF, Channel 61, started as an independent UHF station in 1968, and for a lot of people, it was a breath of fresh air. Sure, there were lots of reruns, but at least they were an alternative to the VHF stations. And there were some live shows, too. All indications were that even though it was based in Parma, WKBF would be a player in the largest TV market in the state. The suburbs were growing, but people still went downtown to shop and see first-run movies. There was still plenty of money in Cleveland.

Jay Berkson, general manager at WKBF, had a plan. He approached the mayor about a weekly series of appearances on Channel 61. Other stations had already talked to Stokes, but the mayor told them he had his hands full running the city. This time, though, something about the offer intrigued him. "Okay," Stokes said. "Let's do it!"

The Cleveland mayor's weekly spot would be three to five minutes twice a week in the middle of the day. Here's the twist: It was on a kids' show! The audience ranged from three to ten

years old. On the *Captain Cleveland* show, Stokes would be discussing urban government, and as *Time* magazine speculated, race
relations. The characters were Captain Cleveland, played by producer John Slowey; Sergeant Sakto; and Private Clem O'Hare, who
would be interviewing the mayor. Clem, by the way, was a puppet.
He sat on Slowey's knee, which made sense, because Slowey was
the ventriloquist.

The weird thing was the microphone setup. These were the days
before wireless lapel mics. Back in the 1960s and most of the 1970s
television used lavalier mics, which hung around your neck like a
noose and were linked to a sound board. You didn't move around
much with one of those on. Oddly, they put a mic around the puppet's neck, too. (At least he didn't have to worry about walking
around with the mic on.)

On the first show, after Stokes took a seat, Clem asked, "What
do I call you? Your highness?" Stokes shook his head with a smile
and said, "Most people use the name Mr. Mayor." They were off and
running. The questions were simple ones a kid might ask, and the
answers could be charming and even insightful.

Clem quizzed the mayor. "Do you own the city?" Stokes assured
Clem he did not; people just trusted him to run it. "Is the policeman
my friend?" The mayor explained that police are indeed friends of
the public, and they made sure everyone's property was as safe as
possible. Clem said, "That's why I can keep my bicycle in front of
my house and no one takes it." Stokes wanted to be as honest as
possible. He said that's what police aimed to do, but also warned
Clem, "Don't do that too much!"

No one was sure how well Stokes could handle the camera,
but he turned to be a natural. His personality and quick wit came
through from the first taping. The guy could ad lib, and the producers expanded his three-minute segments to five and even reran
them during the week. Berkson said, "He's so good, he's unbelievable!" Mayors in other cities had done regularly scheduled TV
spots, including Sam Yorty in Los Angeles and New York's John
Lindsay. But for Cleveland, Stokes was breaking new ground.

What had convinced Stokes to do a kids' show? The closest com-

CARL AND CLEM TALK POLITICS: Cleveland Mayor
Carl Stokes turned down other stations for a regular
spot on a WKBF kids show. He was interviewed every
week by a ventriliquist's dummy named "Private
Clem." *Cleveland Press Collection, Cleveland State University Archives*

parison might have been New York City mayor Fiorello LaGuardia, who had read the comics on radio to New York City's kids in 1945 during a newspaper strike. But television took the concept to a new level. Berkson said it was simple. They told the mayor it was a way to "reach kids before their ideas and prejudices develop." Plus, there might have been just a hint of guilt on Stokes' part. He said, "I've had so little time for my own two children, they might enjoy seeing me on television." Other than on the news shows, of course.

WKBF eventually faded from local TV screens, but what about Stokes? He went on to hold a number of other prominent positions, but first, after leaving the mayor's office, he headed to New York City and in 1972 became the first black news anchorman at WNBC. It's very likely his co-anchor wasn't sitting on someone else's knee.

"Supe's On!"

Marty Sullivan and Superhost

THERE'S A GUY WHO lives in the Pacific Northwest. Oregon to be exact. Way up in the woods. He's been retired for some time and is enjoying his life. He also has a secret identity. Two to be exact.

These days he's Marty Sullivan. But starting in 1969, he took the role of Henry Brookerstein, a mild-mannered director trainee at WUAB TV, Channel 43 in Cleveland. On television, "Henry" would walk onto a set accompanied by an army of production folks showing him scripts and dabbing makeup on him. Then Henry would casually make his way over to a phone booth that was conveniently located in the middle of the studio, drop in a dime, and, POOF! . . . and when the smoke cleared . . . he was Superhost! Bring up the music! Booth announcer, that's your cue. "And with powers far beyond those of ordinary men, Superhost brings you Saturday afternoon! And now, Supe's on!"

He stayed on for a long time, too. Twenty-four years wearing a blue suit of long underwear, red boxing shorts, an equally red nose, a flowing cape and a symbol on his chest that only remotely resembled that other superhero from Cleveland.

Marty Sullivan didn't just wear long underwear around the station. He wore a lot of other hats, too. Audio tech, floor director, booth announcer . . . you name it, Marty did it. But after the show debuted on November 8, 1969, he would always be linked with Superhost.

Marty had a long history in broadcasting before he landed at WUAB. He was raised in Detroit, did a stint in the navy and after he was mustered out, went on to college and a radio career. There were stops in Indiana and Michigan, and then in 1963, a call to

FOR KIDS OF ALL AGES: Marty Sullivan's "Superhost" was aimed at entertaining a very young crowd, but plenty of adults tuned in his Saturday afternoon show as well. *Cleveland Press Collection, Cleveland State University Archives*

the big time, WGAR radio in Cleveland. Marty landed a gig as a street reporter, and there was plenty to report in 1960s Cleveland.

He covered the Hough riots. "I remember it started with just one woman, who happened to be black, throwing a brick," he later told *clevelandseniors.com*. Obviously, there had been a lot more behind the riots than that. Still, Marty was there in the thick of it. One of the guys he met on the street was another radio reporter destined to become a TV host: a young Fred Griffith, then with WIXY and its FM sister station, WDOK. Griffith would go on to become the popular and longtime host of *The Morning Exchange* on WEWS.

For a time Marty worked in advertising, but that wasn't exactly Marty's cup of tea. Then he heard about WUAB. Not everyone had TVs that could pick up UHF, but it was still television, and it was a paycheck. WUAB was a startup operation located in a bowling alley behind Parmatown Mall. This crew flew by the seat of its pants. The announcer's booth was right next to a rest room, and a sign on the rest room door read, "Do not flush when the announcer is announcing."

In 1969, Channel 43 had a show called *Big Beat Dance Party*. Marty was the floor director. He later described it to writer Debbie Hudson as "a lot of aging youngsters who would dance to fifties music." This was the year of Woodstock and Altamont, yet WUAB was trying to attract younger viewers with dinosaur acts like the Four Lads. Clearly, the station didn't know what young viewers were looking for.

At one taping Marty was marking spots for the lighting crew and started doing schtick. Marty later told the website Northeast Ohio Video Hunter: "I was standing there and the director was shouting at me over the headsets that I was unzipped! I must have looked very uncomfortable trying to cover that up! So Ted Bays, the program manager, happened to be in the control room when all this was going on, and everybody in the control room was laughing uproariously; I could hear them on the headset!

"After the show was over, Ted Bays came up and asked me if I wanted to come up with an idea for a show for a character to host a movie. And, that's what I came up with!"

Superhost was born. *Adventure Theater* debuted with a very young, thin Marty Sullivan introducing himself with a high, nasal voice. Dramatic music swells with an announcer's voice stating in dramatic fashion, "Ladies and gentlemen. Due to circumstances completely within our control, Channel 43, in its continuing effort to bring you the best, has spared every expense to bring you . . . Superhost?!" Another offscreen voice answers, "Who?!"

The film cuts to Superhost calmly sitting on a couch with a very agitated guest.

"Superhost! Able to handle difficult guests with ease." He cuts the guy's mic cord.

"Superhost! Able to ad lib for hours." Marty stammers a bit and gives the temperature.

"Superhost! Able to remain impartial." Superhost rambles on loudly at guests about communists before tossing them out of the studio. This went on for a while. You get the idea.

Like Billy Batson turning into Captain Marvel, Marty—as Henry Brookerstein—would change into Superhost (although he did it by saying "Sponsor!" instead of "Shazam!"). Superhost read some phony telegrams, promised top-name guests like Greer Garson and Rory Calhoun, and then introduced the movie, *Attack of the Crab Monsters*. At one point, after an interview with crustacean expert Dr. Henry Pincher, a giant claw came out to grab Superhost.

There were some other skits, and, finally when the show came to an end, Superhost disappeared in a cloud of smoke by saying the magic word, "sponsor." A deep-voiced announcer came on to read the credits (with mostly phony names), and Superhost was on his way.

It was juvenile humor, but Marty knew that. He decided to do juvenile humor better than anyone else. The show would be known by several names, including *Superhost Saturday Mad Theater*.

Supe enjoyed referencing other shows. He would occasionally take calls on screen from "Super Boss," who he claimed wanted his show to be more like "Large Charles and Hooligan" (WJW's *Hoolihan and Big Chuck*). He parodied TV with "The Moronic Woman" (for *The Bionic Woman*) and "Battlestar Ethnica" (for *Battlestar Galactica*), and movies such as "Raiders of the Lost Cause." Marty

BEFORE AND AFTER: Sullivan's Superhost parodied songs and TV shows from the period, including a takeoff on *The Bionic Woman* called "The Moronic Woman." (Try to get that title on a TV show today!) *Cleveland Press Collection, Cleveland State University Archives*

also did a guest spot on *Hee Haw* with Buck Owens and Roy Clark, which was on the WUAB schedule.

Some of Marty's sketches were actually pretty involved. In one skit back in 1979, he played both host and guest with a split screen on "The Morning Eggschange," a lengthy parody of the daytime talk show on Channel 5. In some ways it was an inside joke aimed at his old friend Fred Griffith because Marty was able to mimic Fred's routine so well. Fred liked it and even interviewed Marty as Superhost on *The Morning Exchange*, saying he noticed how Supe would cross and hold his leg the same way Fred did.

It's rare that a local TV station will air segments from a competing station. But you had to actually see Supe's "Morning

Eggschange" to appreciate how clever it was. Right from the start you had the instrumental theme, a beat-up shower head, broken eggs in a pan, broken lace on a tennis shoe, and burnt toast. Just like the real *Morning Exchange* intro, but in the Bizarro world. It segued to a dead-on facsimile of the *Morning Exchange* set including the name on the wall. Then there were the hosts. On the left was Supe as "Joel Host" (for Joel Rose) explaining that Liz was late because of a run-in with a UFO. Right side of the screen was Superhost as Fred teasing what was coming up with his foot planted firmly on his knee. Everyone, of course, is wearing the Superhost costume. Coming up: an interview with an author, Dr. S. Host. Cut to some phony spots, and Bizarro Fred is interviewing the good doctor. His book wasn't out yet, and it was so long since he started working on it that he forgot what it was about.

More phony ads, silly words to live by and the horoscope scroll across the screen. Back with Dr. Host and let's go to the phones. The closer something is to reality the funnier it is, and Supe had the phone routine down pat. One nut after another. "Would you please turn down your TV!" "I want to speak to Dorothy please." And in a nod to Big Chuck Schodowski, "Hello, Ajax liquor store?"

Cut to commercials and it's time for news with Joel Host. He reports on the twenty-two-month debate in the Ohio Legislature that has yet to choose an official state insect . . . but a 100 percent pay raise that was only debated for thirty-seven seconds passed with a unanimous vote.

More phony spots and back to "Morning Eggschange," this time with triple-split screen and "Liz Host" on set. She looks an awful lot like the other two: all are wearing Superhost outfits, but Liz is wearing a wig. She apologizes for her tardiness but explains she was held up shopping for a garbage disposal for her husband, Gary. In real life, Liz Richards was married to radio host Gary Dee in a marriage that played out like a daily soap opera in newspapers and on the air. "Coming up on tomorrow's 'Morning Eggschange,' the original cast of World War II. All of them. See you then!"

Back on the real *Morning Exchange*, after the clip, Fred congratulated Supe for capturing the "subtle nuances" that made him self-conscious for weeks after. Then a few rare serious moments with Superhost as he explained how the character came to be. It turns out that a friend at Channel 8, Don Newmeister, consulted Marty saying the costume could change with the seasons or on special occasions. Maybe a green cape and nose on St. Patrick's Day, or leopard shorts if he's doing a caveman bit. He described Superhost as "super, but bumbling," and said the show had a simple philosophy. "I'm trying to entertain them. What I really think it is that I'm kind of a baby-sitter on Saturday from noon to four to keep the kids quiet. Every once in a while I come in and try to make the commercial seem not so offensive." And the audience? "Strangely enough, though the show is aimed at kiddies I believe the demographics show that over half of them are adults. Closet watchers as it were."

It wasn't the first time Superhost showed up on another channel. There was a skit on Big Chuck and Hoolihan's show on Channel 8 where Chuck ran out of pills to turn him into the recurring character Soul Man. He picked some up from a shady-looking guy on the street, ran into a phone booth, and . . . you guessed it—turned into Superhost.

There's another story with a phone booth. Chuck and John Rinaldi were taping a commercial at Channel 43 and they spotted Superhost's phone booth. An old friend of Chuck's who used to work at WJW, Jerry Jazwa, was now at WUAB. Chuck asked him to help move the booth near the door, and then raced home to get his son's truck. There were plenty of people in on the gag so there was no problem kidnapping the booth. It showed up the next week on *The Big Chuck and Lil' John Show*, and guess who's calling Chuck at home to find out where his phone booth went? They all had a good laugh, Superhost got his booth back, and he kept a close eye on it after that.

The show was usually taped at the last minute, to keep it topical. Marty said, "We tried to keep it toward the end of the week, but we did a lot of commercial work there, so we squeezed it in where

HEY! EYES UP HERE! Sullivan would tape his weekly public service news segment when the crew was ready, and sometimes that was right in the middle of a Superhost taping. Wipe off the make-up, put on a shirt and sport coat, and no one was the wiser. *Cleveland Press Collection, Cleveland State University Archives*

there's time." Sometimes the rush showed. Of course, that was part of the charm of Superhost: So bad it's good!

Another thing about the tapings: Marty would do a weekly five-minute news program—as himself—on Sunday nights. (It was really just community information; this was before the station debuted a nightly news program.) If the Superhost taping was running late and it was time for news, Marty would just wipe off the makeup, put on a jacket and tie and give the headlines. From the waist down he was still Superhost!

Superhost parodied familiar commercials for recording artists

Boxcar Willie and Slim Whitman with "Caboose Supe" and "Fat Whitman." One of his most popular skits was based on C.W. McCall's trucker song "Convoy." The skit looked like it was directed by Ed Wood, the low-budget artiste responsible for *Plan 9 from Outer Space*, with a semi cab made from cardboard, toy trucks, and a chorus line of truckers. Even so, it was a fan favorite to the end.

The end came in 1989. One Saturday, Superhost closed his show teasing a big announcement the following week. It was almost twenty years to the day since his first show, and Marty had grown thinner on top and thicker in the middle. He opened the following week in the usual way and then, standing in front of an elaborate theater marquee he used for his set, Supe dropped the bomb. This would be the last *Superhost* show. Ever. He said, "It was a decision by Super Boss and the great brains in the front office." Then it was movies and film shorts as usual, and when the end came, Superhost put on a straw boater and picked up a red bag. The nasal voice was still there, but you could tell this wasn't easy. "I want to thank you for all your kindness all these years. You've been wonderful, and Northeast Ohio is a class act. So there!" Supe walked through the door, and locked the theater behind him. He paused again and looked into the camera. "I would like to take this opportunity to thank each and every one of you for tuning in over the years. The last twenty years have been great, mainly due to you. And now, I have to try to find my way to Krypton." His thumb went out, there was a screech of tires, and Superhost got his ride.

Marty held it together, and then it hit him. "Taping the last show, I thought I'd get emotional, and I was doing pretty good," he later told the Video Hunter website. "And then we were breaking down the set and I was walking out, and one of the crew members said, 'How you doing?' and that kinda got to me. Then it all came to me in a rush: this was the end."

It got to us, too. Never again would we start our Saturday afternoon with "Gimme dat shoe!"

"Weather and sportscasters look like real people."

Al Roker in Cleveland

AL ROKER WASN'T ONE of those guys who saw his calling right away. Television fascinated him when he was growing up in New York City, but he didn't think it would be a career. But he started getting TV experience early on. At the Xavier Military Academy, which he attended on a scholarship, he was director of the school's daily closed-circuit newscast. He was happy to work behind the scenes. At the State University of New York at Oswego he studied communications but took a class in meteorology because it seemed an easy way to fulfill his science requirement. "I didn't go to college to strain myself," he said.

Al picked things up quickly, though, and that, combined with his over-the-top personality, led a SUNY professor to suggest that Al try out for a weekend weather spot at a CBS-TV station in Syracuse. Still in his sophomore year at Oswego, Al would have a 100-mile commute every time he pulled a shift. The job paid $15 per forecast. He got it, and it led to Al taking more classes in meteorology. By his senior year, when the full-time weather guy suddenly quit, Al had the inside track on the job.

Welcome to the sixty-seventh largest TV market in the country! It turned out to be an excellent training ground.

Al was not the typical weathercaster viewers had become used to on television. He described his style in those days to a *Plain Dealer* reporter as "Crazier. I was a lunatic. I really was nuts. I was like a Tasmanian devil!" Years later Al told David Letterman that he had always wanted to "be a 'toon." In his interview with *The*

Plain Dealer, he said, "Wouldn't that be great if you could really do that, if you could twirl around like that? I mean, wouldn't it be great if people could be like cartoon characters? You could jump out a window and go splat on the sidewalk, then pop back up and walk away. I'd love it." He added with a smile, "You gotta understand. I'm a looney 'toon."

Al felt pretty comfortable in that spot, too. He told a *Cleveland Press* reporter, "Anchor people still look better than the weather and sports people. Weather and sportscasters look like real people. That's why people like us."

After Al Roker arrived in Cleveland, he would occasionally be seen nationally on NBC. Here's some trivia for you: he even got a shot during prime time . . . when the show *Real People* pulled into the train station in Cleveland.

But we're getting ahead of ourselves. Just six months out of SUNY/Oswego, Al got an offer from WTTG in Washington. A large market offer already? He'd have been crazy to have turned it down. Al would later say, "I gotta admit I didn't listen very carefully during the interview. They told me they had the number-one newscast at 10:00 p.m., and I got all excited. It wasn't until the plane ride back that I realized they had the *only* 10:00 p.m. newscast in Washington." That didn't mean big ratings.

In the two years Al was at WTTG, the station struggled, although Al got favorable reviews. How bad were the numbers? Al remembered it this way: "We were number one in Arlington Cemetery. We had an older demographic."

Well, you want the news before you go to bed, and sometimes age determines what time you hit the hay. Al's audience went to bed six hours after the dinner hour—and they ate at four o'clock.

Fortunately, Al met an old pro who would be a major professional influence. Willard Scott had been one of radio's "Joy Boys" in Washington and had made an easy transition to TV at the NBC affiliate there. He told Al, "You're good, but calm down. You'll last a lot longer." Those words stayed with Al, and Willard remained a lifelong friend. They were so close that years later, during a visit

SKETCH COMEDY: WKYC's Al Roker would often use his cartooning skills to liven up his weather reports. *Cleveland Press Collection, Cleveland State University Archives*

to Cleveland TV, Willard would take off his toupee and pop it on Al's head. Al continued to refine his on-air image, looking for a bigger audience.

In Cleveland, WKYC, Channel 3, was going through a rebuilding process that rivaled the woeful Cleveland Indians. New faces year after year. An NBC scout suggested to the station that they look at Al Roker. He was only twenty-four years old when he got the call from WKYC, but said he got the gig because he looked thirty-five or forty. That's because he said he was "weathered." (Groan!) News director Dick Lobo was looking for a weathercaster who would add some spice to the cast. He told *The Plain Dealer*, "I'd like to find someone who is a professional weatherman, but is a personality as well. I can't out-Goddard Goddard; that's for sure." Dick Goddard had long been a marquee name at

Channel 8, and it was speculated that if he ever left the station, the ratings would go with him.

WKYC station management asked Al if he would be willing to work in Cleveland, and he really didn't have much of a reaction. He remembered, "I really hadn't heard anything about Cleveland. I didn't know any Cleveland jokes." He would learn plenty in short order. Al looked up Cleveland history in an almanac and found out about the racial tension, the Cuyahoga River fire, the fire that lit up Mayor Perk's hair, and it didn't get any better from there. He tore out the page so his wife wouldn't see it because WKYC was owned by NBC in the nation's tenth largest market . . . and he really wanted out of WTTG.

Al remembered his first impressions of Cleveland in a newspaper interview. "When I came in for my interview, I came in at night and they drove me past Republic Steel. I thought, 'My God. This is Dante's Inferno!'" This was going to be a hard sell getting his wife to move here. Still, he accepted the offer and bags were packed.

When Al announced the job up north, his friends asked, "Cleveland? Are you nuts?" Even so, he said he liked the challenge forecasting North Coast weather. "You don't get much lake effect off of the Tidal Basin, unless Wilbur Mills is there." You might recall that Mills was the disgraced Arkansas congressman who was caught with a stripper named Fanne Foxe when police stopped him for speeding. She tried to escape by diving into the Basin. That pretty much ended Mills' career in Congress.

This new guy at WKYC was also a talented cartoonist, though he admitted it was "more for fun than profit." Al had used his cartoons in his weather reports in Washington, but he was good enough that WKYC was worried that they would distract from his forecast. Instead, Al suggested the station install a new color radar system that would dress up the weather with big, bright maps. He nicknamed it "Fred."

Cleveland took to Al Roker right away. People would call him at the station to compliment his on-air work. He said that was incredible because in Washington, "They call to tell you you're doing a lousy job. People there seem to thrive on failure." Right after moving into his home in Shaker Heights, a neighbor stopped by with a loaf of freshly baked wheat bread. As Al put it, "In Washington, you would think there was a bomb in the bread!" News anchor Amanda Arnold nicknamed him "Obie Roke."

Network executives at NBC saw star potential early on, but Al seemed content in Cleveland. He didn't like WKYC's third-place finish, though, because he knew they were better than that. Part of the reason for the low ratings was the station's revolving door. "People in Cleveland don't like change," he pointed out. "They don't like to see new people popping up all the time."

People did like Al Roker, though. Remember what Al said about the sports and weather spots? That's where personality and character shine, and he sure stepped up to the plate. It was there right from the start. Al walked on the WKYC set in January 1979, and showed he knew how to get attention. Low-key was not the term to describe Al Roker. Props? You got 'em! Jokes? Plenty, and sharp as a tack, too. Impersonations? Al had Walter Cronkite down pat, and could even do Michael Conrad from *Hill Street Blues*. "It's going to be wet tonight so . . . HEY! Be careful out there!"

One of Al's great off–the-cuff remarks happened after a report by syndicated writer Jeff Greenfield suggested that the old kids' puppet show *Howdy Doody* had been responsible for much of the campus unrest back in the 1960s. Greenfield claimed—in jest— that Howdy had taught kids not to trust adults.

Al saw an opportunity. He did the weather and, playing it straight, looked into the camera and said he'd learned that "Howdy Doody grew up, gained a little weight, dyed his hair, bleached out his freckles, and is now working as an anchorman on a 5:30 newscast right here in Cleveland!" He started to talk faster, stood up from his chair and pointed his finger in the air. Then he put his arm around anchorman Tom Sweeney and, imitating Howdy, yelled out, "Buffalo Bob! Hey lookit! Buffalo Bob!"

With Al, you got weather and a stage show. The problem was, how do you follow him?

WKYC's "A" TEAM: Roker was part of a Channel 3 news team that included Mona Scott and Doug Adair, who were a couple off the screen as well. *Cleveland Press Collection, Cleveland State University Archives*

There was some speculation that people followed him in other ways. Some TV critics saw Al's influence on WJW's Dick Goddard (who, coincidentally, was also an amateur cartoonist). As Goddard's on-air style got a little more casual, some said it was a reaction to the competition.

Al Roker was a true star in Northeast Ohio. Strangers thought they knew him, and privacy was something he had to give up. He'd walk through a restaurant and someone would stop him to ask, "What's the weather?" (Like they were the first to think that up.) Al would smile, shake their hand or pat them on the back and say, "Stick your head out the window!" No one was ever offended.

Sometimes the planets align, and that's what happened for Al in November 1983. The weekend weather guy at WNBC in New York had left the previous spring, and Al's contract at WKYC was coming up. He looked into the New York job, and by June, the die was cast. Even though he truly enjoyed life in Cleveland, Al was glad to be planning a move home to New York. He wanted to be closer to his family.

Al was a true entertainer, but he was a weatherman first, and took that job very seriously. The fun could wait until after the important stuff, and he put in a lot of extra hours on the job and wore a lot of different hats. He also did daily forecasts on WGCL-FM, filled in as host on Dave Patterson's talk show, and got out to meet the public whenever he could. He credited his dad for his work ethic. Soon his parents would see him on local TV.

Al packed his dog Schnoodle into the car and said goodbye to Cleveland. He went on to a stellar career on the network, with a long stay on *Today* and even an appearance on an episode of *Seinfeld*.

Every now and then, he would see someone from Cleveland, and once, he had a very strange encounter with one of the town's most notable anti-heroes.

Harvey Pekar made a huge name for himself with his *American Splendor* comic book series, which told the story of his life in Cleveland. But the real-life Harvey was even more entertaining, and he became a regular on David Letterman's show on NBC. The show taped late in the afternoon, and for one taping, in 1987, Harvey was on the set when Dave suggested they take a walk around the studios.

WNBC's *Live on Five* was airing in a nearby studio and, as you might guess from the show's name, it was live. Dave and Harvey walked in to see anchors Sue Simmons and Jack Cafferty and, sure enough, Al Roker, all sitting at the desk. Dave interrupted their show to introduce everyone, but Harvey beamed in on Al. Dave pretty much took over *Live on Five*, cracking jokes and explaining why they were there. Meanwhile, Harvey was talking a hundred miles an hour to Al about Cleveland. As Dave pulled Harvey away so they could continue the show, you could hear Harvey asking Al about Wally Kinnan and Dick Goddard.

It's hard to get away from Cleveland. Even in New York!

"We told everybody they're going to be offended."

WEWS Takes Heat for Grisly Footage

You don't have a lot of time to make decisions with breaking news. If you make the wrong choice you chalk it up to experience—as the old saying goes, "Hindsight is 20/20." Sometimes, though, what you see is impossible to forget.

In January 1987, Pennsylvania state treasurer R. Budd Dwyer called a news conference. Cameras were rolling and, after a brief statement, Dwyer pulled a .357 Magnum from a bag, put it in his mouth and pulled the trigger. The cameras caught everything, including the horrifying conclusion. The footage was fed to affiliates, and most ran the story but cut away before the trigger was pulled. WEWS in Cleveland did not. It aired the complete footage, uncut—and did they ever hear about it! Yet not only did they run the whole grisly tape at the dinner hour at six, they reran it at eleven. Here it comes!

The footage is still available on YouTube, and it's no less frightening today than the day it happened. People cried out to Dwyer, begging him to put down the gun. Before anyone could rush him, he opened fire. It's amazing the videographers were able to continue taping. It's that horrifying.

Public outcry over the broadcast was deafening, and news director Dick Tuininga was on the hot seat. The switchboards couldn't handle the flood of calls. It was all anyone talked about, and people wanted answers. About a month later, after tempers and emotions had cooled a bit, Tuininga came forward to discuss the decision to air the footage. It had been his call to show it, and he addressed two separate forums to give his side of the story. He spoke to the Radio-TV Council of Greater Cleveland, Inc., and the Cleveland chapter of the Society of Professional Journalists, Sigma Delta Chi. There were plenty of media there, including *The Plain Dealer*, which reported the details.

Tuininga admitted, "I will probably reflect on that decision for the rest of my career. It will probably produce an emotional rush, and I'm not sure it will be a pleasant one." Yes, he said, WEWS did air the footage, as did three other stations across the country. He said Channel 5 also aired a warning: "We told everybody they were going to be offended. Then we retold them they would be offended.

"Then I wondered, 'Why are they offended?'"

He said he hadn't done it for higher ratings In fact, if anything he expected to lose viewers. As it turned out, the broadcast had no effect on the numbers that night.

It did have an effect on Tuiniga's incoming mail. He received hundreds of letters and, as might be expected, they ran six to one against his decision. Plenty of people disagreed with running the footage.

One of those was his wife, who wouldn't speak with him for several days afterward. Then there was the WEWS management. Station manager Don Webster stressed it had not been a management decision to show the uncut footage. Most of the station's managers had been out of town when it happened.

Webster questioned Tuininga's judgment, saying, "I think it was just a bad decision and, if it were up to me, I wouldn't have done it." Yet he also gave Tuininga a vote of confidence: "We didn't cut his head off. He's a good guy, and we stand behind him."

Tuininga said many in the newsroom didn't understand his decision, and the anchors had "strong opinions." But they didn't question the choice to run it again in the eleven o'clock newscast.

Why did Tuininga run the whole clip instead of the edited version fed by ABC News? He said Dwyer was a public official, and "suicide does not end by fading to black. It ends in death." He had specifically looked for the entire footage, which had been available from Group W broadcasting. Tuininga also said he didn't want to "edit a real-life situation." As he put it: "I don't care to have ABC in New York or Los Angeles making that decision for us." Many thought the network would have used a little more discretion.

One of the news professionals attending the SPJ event was Thomas Greer, *The Plain Dealer's* managing editor, who chose not to run photos of Dwyer with the gun in his mouth or the aftermath. He said the most graphic photos "suggested a kind of sensationalism that I didn't think was necessary." Greer did admit that might have been a more difficult decision had the subject been an official from Northeast Ohio.

At that time, newspaper columnist Dick Feagler was doing commentary for WKYC. He moderated the SPJ event and, surprisingly, said he agreed with Tuininga. But leave it to Feagler to find humor is a tough situation. When callers contacted him to complain, he said he agreed with them and "I damned Mr. Tuininga and urged them to watch us!"

Not Making Many Friends

Investigative Reporters

HEY KIDS! WANT A career with endless hours, physical threats, and lawyers breathing down your neck? Have we got a job for you: investigative reporter!

All kidding aside, this is one tough racket. A lot of stations began doing investigative reports in the 1970s after Bob Woodward and Carl Bernstein took down Richard Nixon in the *Washington Post*. (Geraldo Rivera was one of the early reporters getting into people's faces on television.) But it takes a special person to do that job for any length of time.

Cleveland has seen a lot of solid investigative reporters on TV. Bill Sheil, Lorrie Taylor, Dave Summers, Ted Hart, Ron Regan . . . They'll tell you just how difficult the job is, and how great the pressure is to produce. You say you're an investigative reporter? Show us. Especially during sweeps.

David Lee Miller got a lot of attention back in the mid-1980s at WKYC Channel 3. But doing news is like feeding a hungry monster. More, more, and more . . . and when that's done, you can start all over again. Miller was doing WKYC's investigative work, but news director Ron Bilek didn't think he was delivering enough product. When *The Plain Dealer* asked why Miller's contract wasn't renewed, Bilek flat-out said, "That's our option. If your guy is not grinding out the material and you're up against an established investigative team [Channel 8's], after a while you start to lose ground." The search for a replacement for Miller was slow, too. Bilek said he wasn't impressed by the tapes he was seeing, claiming, "In TV, there are a lot of people who like to be called

TRUTH CAN BE DANGEROUS: Investigative reporters like
Paul Orlousky can often be targeted by folks on both sides
of the law. One report got Orlousky written up for phony
tickets . . . and an arrest warrant soon after! *Paul Orlousky*

investigative reporters, but they can't do it." There was also some
really tough competition.

Then they hired Paul Orlousky.

Paul has been a fixture on Cleveland TV for decades. You make
a name with hard work, and his stuff at WKYC really stood out.
One notable report was a piece he did on police officers loafing on
the job at Deaconess Hospital. It was the story that just kept on
giving . . .

Someone gave Paul a tip about on-duty cops taking very long
breaks at Deaconess. He had it on a piece of paper in his back
pocket and thought he would check it out when he got a chance.
Not long after that, the chance came.

TV news reporter victim of forged traffic ticket

Judge calls phony ticket scam 'incredibly stupid'

Two officers suspected of issuing false tickets

Paul and a crew were checking out an accident on I-480 at Pearl Road. That didn't turn out to be anything for them, but they were close enough to Deaconess Hospital to stop by and take a look. As they rolled up, they saw seven empty police cars and all the cops sitting in a break room. About a week later, producer Greg Lockhart and videographer Pete Miller sat in a surveillance van in 95-degree heat, timing the cops—and found they were taking four- and five-hour breaks! Paul came in to do some interviews, and the stories ran on Thursday and Friday.

As a result of the WKYC report, seventeen of thirty-five officers were suspended. However, Paul had run afoul of an unwritten rule: you don't mess with the cops. One of the cops called Paul a lowlife; another yelled obscenities and wanted to fight him at him at the Galleria. Then came the traffic tickets.

This is where the story takes a weird turn. Two cops (who were not named in the WKYC report) who were working together in the same car both wrote tickets that Sunday saying Paul had run a red light and driven 42 mph in a 35 mph zone. It was the Sunday before Christmas. Paul had been in church and nowhere near the downtown locations where the phony citations supposedly were issued. The cops also didn't sign their names.

There was another officer they didn't like who worked out of that same car, and they had used her ticket book—to mess with her, too. The copies that would have been given to motorist—Paul— were thrown in the trash. Hard to defend yourself in court if you don't know you've been cited! Here's the rub: If you don't show up in court, after thirty days a warrant is issued for your arrest. Thirty days after that, you're listed on police computers nationwide as a fugitive! Had Paul had been stopped—anywhere—for a minor traffic offense, he would have been hauled away to jail!

One evening, Paul was walking out of the WKYC building on East Sixth Street and he met a councilman he knew who said, "Hey! You're in trouble. There's a warrant for your arrest!" Huh?

Here's the way Paul remembers it. "I gave a call to Benny Bonnano, the clerk of courts. Told him what happened, and he let out a little laugh and said I should hang on. Bonnano checked the warrants and his voice took a different tone. 'You'd better get down here!'"

Paul walked into Bonnano's office and Bonnano handed him a piece of paper and said, "Sign your name." He then pulled out the tickets, and saw that not only did the signatures not match; the cops had misspelled Paul's name. These obviously were phony tickets. Now, it was time to round up the culprits. Easy enough. The names were on the tickets.

There was a trial, and you can be sure Channel 3 covered it. The judge called the forged tickets "incredibly stupid," and the two policemen had to come clean. They pleaded guilty to a laundry list of charges, including perjury, forgery, falsification of records, and even uttering (entering phony documents). On to the sentencing.

The scene in the courtroom was emotional. The officers' wives were crying, the cops looked nervous, and the judge was not happy. Before he handed down the sentence, the judge asked whether anyone had anything to say, and he looked right at Paul. "Nobody was hurt," Paul said. "It's resolved. Give them a break." The break was eighteen months' probation and one hundred fifty hours of community service.

All in all, it was not the kind of experience that endears you to the safety forces. Or does it? A few months later, one of the cops rang up Paul to say the city was messing with his pension. Could he do a story?

A couple of other reports from the early years really stand out. John Demjanjuk was the Seven Hills auto worker accused of being the infamous Nazi death camp guard "Ivan the Terrible." His case dragged on for years, not only his extradition to Israel and his trial, but his eventual return to the U.S. Paul Orlousky had covered the trial in Israel, and even reported from Tel Aviv and Jerusalem. He estimated he had spent at least eight hundred hours on the Demjanjuk case, so he knew the story well. In October 1993, just after his return to the U.S., Demjanjuk went into hiding for three weeks. Nobody knew where he was, but there was a watch to see when he would return to his house in Northeast Ohio.

On the 7th, Paul got a tip that Demjanjuk would be delivered to his home that day at noon. Problem was, he got the tip at 11:30 a.m.! The videographer he was working with was Joe Butano, known as "the Cowboy." Joe was a big guy with lots of gold chains, a great sense of humor, and not afraid to offer advice on a story. The two raced to stake out the Demjanjuk house, and it looked like a military operation was in progress. The bomb squad did a once-over, and there were dogs and people looking all over the property. They didn't know whether the tip was right, but they had to set up cameras so that they wouldn't be seen, just in case.

Paul remembers, "Joe thought we should just go up to the door, but I said we should wait. 'No, Paul, let's go knock on the door.' 'Joe, let's just be ready.' 'Paul, I'm telling you . . .'"

Suddenly, "Joe, look! He's coming!" Less than two minutes after they had arrived on Meadow Lane, two Seven Hills police cars appeared. Inside were the chief, a lieutenant, two detectives, . . . and John Demjanjuk! Joe scrambled to get some video, but it happened so fast that he couldn't set up properly for a light balance. They did get some tape, but it was just a shadowy image. Even so, it was a scoop for Channel 3: the only time Demjanjuk would be confronted by a local reporter after his return home.

Videographers almost always dress casually, but that day, Paul was dressed down, too—jeans, a zippered jacket, and looking very comfortable. Not his usual street clothes.

Demjanjuk was rushed inside the house. They walked over and knocked on the door, but got no answer. Paul left his business card in the door, and as they walked away, three more police cars rolled up. The police chief, John Fechko, made it clear that he didn't appreciate them waiting for Demjanjuk to arrive. Exclusive or not, he let Paul and Joe know: "My opinion, none of you [reporters] are welcome. I am advising you, one time, that you have committed a criminal violation. If it happens again, I will arrest you." Joe rolled tape so the other stations would get the message when they saw it on WKYC that night.

Sometimes the teases were as good as the stories. Once, Paul had the goods on some police who spent a lot of time at the Hough Bakery on East Ninth Street. The story was titled "Creampuff Cops," and newspaper ads read: "It's tough to take a bite out of crime with a mouthful of doughnut!"

There was a weird story once from Bedford Heights. It happened in the early 1990s. A worker at a crematorium said the guy who burned the bodies at a cemetery there would save gas and money by not completing the jobs. It took a lot of energy to completely destroy the bones, so the guy would give only some of the cremains to the family. Then he would store the skeletons in fifty-gallon oil drums and dump them in graves before the concrete vault was dropped. The relatives were none the wiser.

Stakeout time again, this time with videographer Pete Miller. Stakeouts usually mean long hours of waiting for the right shot, and it was no different this time. The pair waited for a couple of days and then, pay dirt! A worker drove up to an open grave in a golf cart with three barrels. Pete and Paul got video from across the street, moved closer to see the grave, and then Paul did his report while showing skeletal remains. Hip sockets, leg bones . . . he even held up a shoulder blade! There was public outcry and talk that the state legislature would take action. They didn't, and nothing happened to the people dumping the bones. Very frustrating. Oh, and the name of the report? "Rest in Pieces." (Like you didn't see that coming!)

When you're sitting on a hot story, you roll the dice. Paul once sat on a report too long and Channel 5 broke it, but what a story! In 1979, Michael Levine kidnapped and murdered Julius Kravitz, the former owner of the Pick-n-Pay supermarket chain, and seriously wounded Kravitz' wife, Georgene. He was found not guilty by reason of insanity and sentenced to a mental health center in Dayton.

Fourteen years later he was back on the streets, released from the hospital, and looking to start over in Northeast Ohio. Levine was even spotted in the Flats. Paul tailed him for three days and got footage of Levine leaving a very nice apartment, bowling, dining out, and even going to a health club. The investigative team didn't want Levine to know he was being trailed, and when it was time to move in, somehow they lost him. Figuring it was waste of time, they decided to call it a night and went to a bar for chicken wings. While they were waiting for the wings, Paul's cameraman nodded to Paul that he should quietly disappear because Levine had walked in and was standing right behind him. Even so, Levine was out and about and they would track him down for the interview.

It happened on day three in Kettering, and Levine agreed to answer a few questions. Fifteen minutes later, they had an exclusive, but decided not to air it right away. This time it worked against them. Ted Hart at Channel 5 had found Levine's apartment, too, and had left a business card. Levine phoned the station and set up a time to sit down with Hart and Ted Henry. Then the bombs started dropping.

As Paul Orlousky told *The Plain Dealer*, most people had no idea what Levine sounded like, and that included the county common pleas judge who presided over the case, John Angelotta. Levine didn't want to discuss the Kravitz case because he was saving that interview to promote a book he was writing. Seriously? Then he told Ted Henry he was bitter that he had to do fourteen years, and was able to kill again. He also thought comments that he had gotten away with murder were "a cheap shot." But it's what he said next that really got attention:

Levine claimed the judge had declared him not guilty by reason of insanity as a favor to his attorney, Jerry Milano, who was a friend. Wow! Next stop, Judge John Angelotta, and Channel 8 "Fact Finder" Tom Meyer was right on the case.

The two names that have pretty much defined TV investigative reporting in Cleveland were Carl Monday and Tom Meyer. The two worked together as Channel 8's "I-Team" for a couple of years before Tom took on his new role. Judge Angelotta refused comment to both *The Plain Dealer* and Paul Orlousky, and chances are, he wasn't looking to give anyone else a scoop.

Tom recalls, "I called Judge Angelotta and told his bailiff specifically why we wanted to get his comments. It's only when the judge or the bailiff failed to return multiple calls that I decided to try to catch up with him at the courthouse."

TV is a business where the pros will go to any length for even a few seconds of video. Tom asked Angelotta off camera if he would talk with him as he left his courtroom, but the judge ignored him and kept walking. These were obviously serious allegations by Levine, and people wanted to know Angelotta's reaction. The silent treatment wasn't going to cut it. As a last resort, Tom set up at the Justice Center cafeteria. When the judge stopped in for a bite, Tom made his move.

The judge didn't say a word, but his actions got his message across. He pushed the camera away, threw his tray of food at Tom, covered his face, and headed for the elevator. Tom finished his report wearing Angelotta's lunch. That was some meal, too. Mashed potatoes, some kind of mystery meat, blueberry pie . . . and videographer Ron Mounts captured it all on tape.

This promised to be some good TV! Tom says, "An assistant manager, Grant Zalba, viewed it, liked it, and decided to lead the newscast that night with the story." Even so, orders came down from the front office that the interview would not air again. And it didn't—at least not until it was played during a hearing to determine whether the judge should be sanctioned for tossing the food tray. He was lucky he didn't get a dry cleaning bill on top of it!

* * *

Investigative stories often take some weird turns, and they don't get much weirder than this next one. Consumer news is fertile ground for investigative reports. After all, viewers are consumers. In the days before Angie's List, when hiring a contractor you were gambling on whether or not it was a reputable one. Most people don't know much about furnaces except that they want theirs in good shape before winter comes. So furnace inspection crews tend to be very busy inspecting heating systems in the fall. Problem is, some of them want to make sure they'll have plenty of work afterward, too.

Tom Meyer decided to do a series about shady furnace repair men. First he had to find some. He hid some cameras in the window wells in the basement of his house in University Heights, where he was living at the time. He had a female producer act as the homeowner, and scheduled eight repair people to stop by through the day, ninety minutes apart. Of course, one guy came late and met another repairman in the driveway, and they both drove away mad, but there were plenty more who showed up on time. Every now and then, the producer would walk downstairs to see what was happening.

Here's the deal: The furnace was in perfect shape, so Tom would have the goods on anyone who claimed otherwise. In fact, you can hear one of the repairmen on tape muttering, "Goddamn, is this furnace clean!"

At the end of the day Tom had a big pile of tapes to sift through, and he looked forward to a long day in the editing booth. Now, think about it. Eight guys doing furnace inspections. Talk about tedium! After a while, Tom just sat there with his face in his hand, writing down numbers from the tape deck's time code. At one point he started to doze off when something woke him up quickly. One of the repair guys dropped his tool box . . . and then he dropped his pants! Nude from the waist down, and instead of working on the furnace, he started working on himself!

Word got around the newsroom quickly and pretty soon, it was like clowns stuffing themselves in a phone booth. Virgil Dominic was the news director, and he ran over asking, "What's the commotion?" He rubbed his eyes in disbelief. This was a double-edged sword. On one side, Tom had an unbelievable story. On the other, this creep was in his basement! Not only that, the producer who was acting as his wife had just missed the show when she went into the basement to check on him.

The story ran and, sure enough, it included some shady repair guys, including the guy with the hand party. Tom named the companies, too. He blurred the guy's face and body, and Tom tagged his report stressing homeowners had to be careful who they hired. He also mentioned the "despicable, X-rated act" done by one of the repair men.

After the story ran, Tom got a call from one of the companies, and the guy was livid. How dared he malign their company's name and employees? Tom came right back at him. "Be glad I didn't mention where that one guy worked!" A pause. The company rep said in a much calmer tone, "Please don't tell me that was our guy." Surprise! The company spokesman asked whether he could bring the repairman in the next day to explain everything, and even offered to fire him on the spot. Nobody wanted that, but the door was open. Sure enough, they showed up the next day and the repair guy admitted he was "sexually excited by flames." Good thing they didn't meet in the station's smoking lounge.

No word what happened to the worker, but pray he didn't find a job with the fire department. Tom's wife saw the report, and when he got home, she said he had his own inspection to do. There's the basement.

As a TV investigative reporter you tend not to make many friends among the people you interview. When Tom was at WOIO, he did a report about then-Mayor Jane Campbell's husband, Hunter Morrison, driving to his job at Youngstown State University in a city-owned car. A nice car, too—a fully loaded 2003 Ford Explorer that was top-of-the-line all the way. It was a 180-mile round trip to

YSU and back, and here's the catch: Morrison didn't work for the city. Plus, the mayor was threatening layoffs in the fire and police departments, as many as two hundred fifty across the board.

While Mayor Campbell was waiting for her own car and driver, Tom caught up with her to ask what was going on. She was not happy. "It's a family car, a city car that was part of the mayor's compensation package!" Then the mayor's driver, Kevin Berry, who was also her bodyguard, stepped in. He slammed the car door closed and almost hit Tom in the process.

Campbell eventually turned in her husband's keys, but there were still three cars assigned to her and her family, and Tom kept an eye on how they were used, especially in light of hundreds of city layoffs. Turns out, another officer drove the mayor's kids around and spent a lot of time on the road over a two-year period that included baseball games, skiing, guitar lessons, and lacrosse camps.

There's more. That same officer sometimes drove the kids and their friends to Michigan, West Virginia, and to shopping sprees in Pennsylvania and New York City. You read that right. They drove to New York City! That driver made $28,000 in overtime in 2003 alone.

The travel continued even outside the car pool.

Mayor Campbell accepted an invitation to visit Ireland with Craig Tame, who was the head of health and public safety. The trip was intended to celebrate western Ireland's link with Cleveland. The mayor's driver, Kevin Berry, had the chance to tag along. Let's keep in mind that the city was in a financial crisis. One laid-off cop said the department was calling tow trucks to jump start dead batteries in zone cars. Even so, Campbell and company headed to the Old Sod. The mayor said the trip was funded by their friends in Ireland, but it turns out that might not have covered the whole four days for everyone. Indeed, some of Berry's trip was paid for with $1,300 from the Law Enforcement Trust Fund, money set aside for police training and equipment used for investigations. It was a very nice trip, too. Along with the scenery, Berry took in eighty-four hours of overtime for an additional $2,000. He was already one of the city's top overtime earners, ranking twenty-ninth in 2003 with $33,000 in overtime.

Tame said he paid for the trip out of his own pocket, but what about Berry? He ended up billing the city $1,300 for the trip. Campbell said Berry had been asked to come along to provide security, even though a local Irish expert named John O'Brien would later say the area where they stayed was virtually crime-free. Tom Meyer also discovered that Berry had stayed in a bed and breakfast down the road from where the mayor had set up camp . . . but if there was an emergency, he was only fifteen minutes away! He apparently made quite an impression at the B&B, too. They told Tom, "Kevin ate us out of house and home . . . Tell him we said hi." Something had to be done.

Mayor Campbell banned Tom Meyer and Channel 19 from City Hall. No one was to speak to him or to WOIO. That ended up in court, with the city claiming Tom's reports had compromised the safety of the mayor's family. The city also introduced a brief video clip of the kids shot from a distance, although an argument was made that the mayor herself brought her kids in front of cameras. Ultimately it didn't really matter, as Mayor Campbell was eventually voted out of office.

Tom moved on as well—to WKYC. That's where he aired one of his most disturbing reports ever.

Hope Steffey was in a fight with a cousin and got beaten up pretty badly. Another cousin called 911, and a Stark County sheriff's deputy raced to the scene. It got real ugly from there, and much of it was recorded on surveillance video. When the deputy arrived on the scene, he saw a handful of Steffey's hair lying in a clump on the ground, and she had a bald spot. Needless to say she was pretty upset, and the deputy told her to calm down. Steffey was inconsolable. An altercation ensued, and the deputy ended up slamming Steffey's face down onto the hood of the police car, cracking one of her teeth.

The deputy pinned her and yelled, "Are you going to stop?" Then he twisted her arm up behind her neck, picked her up, and smashed her into the road. Steffey weighed only 125 pounds, and when she was face-first in the dirt, the deputy jumped in the air and landed on top of her back. He put a knee in her back and shouted again, "Are you going to stop?"

Blood was everywhere. Steffey couldn't breathe, and the deputy finally eased up after the cousin screamed, "You're hurting her!" He handcuffed Steffey and put her in the back of the cruiser. At his point, it was far from over.

They ended up at the sheriff's office for questioning, and the deputy left Steffey in the car while he spoke to a colleague. He came back to tell her if she did what they said, she would probably go home that evening. They put Steffey in a little room, face against the wall. Seven deputies were there, two of them male, and they asked whether she had any sharp objects. She said, "No!" and they took her to a jail cell.

While answering questions from a nurse, Steffey heard one of the deputies say something, and then her legs were knocked out from under her. Again, she was face down on a concrete floor, and this time three other deputies joined in to hold her head, ankles, and legs. She was stripped naked, and Steffey later said she felt she was being raped. Then the female deputies left the cell, Steffey's arm was pulled up behind her back, and she screamed in pain.

If this was considered a strip search, it didn't follow the letter of the law. Ohio State Code 2933.32 states, "A body cavity search or strip search shall be conducted by a person or persons who are of the same sex as the person who is being searched, and the search shall be conducted in a manner and in a location that permits only search person or persons who are physically conducting the search and the person who is being searched to observe the search."

Eventually, Steffey was handcuffed again, they folded back her legs and she was tossed, nude and covered with bruises, into a jail cell. She stayed there for six hours, and covered her genitals with toilet paper to prevent male deputies from seeing her private parts when they made their rounds. They hadn't even given her a blanket.

Steffey was not given medical care during that time. Eventually she was told that she was being charged with resisting arrest and disorderly conduct. Remember, the deputies had been called by the cousin because Steffey was a crime victim. She had not been allowed phone calls to family or an attorney. They did later give her a sleeveless vest to wear, but she was still naked from the waist down. Yet another indignation as she walked through the police station past male deputies to a booking room.

And much of this was on video that was obtained by Steffey's attorney and ended up with Tom Meyer.

Tom ran a story about Steffey's treatment, and the resulting case against the deputies went to a grand jury. You'd better be sitting down for this part. It was determined that after reviewing the evidence, the Stark County deputies would not face indictments because their actions were a precaution against suicide. Also, although they had so-called "suicide suits" for prisoners, Steffey was considered too dangerous to be issued one. Despite the apparent violation of the strip search, it was also determined that there was no policy preventing men from stripping women's clothes off during suicide prevention. Steffey insisted she was not suicidal and was not told she could remove her own clothing.

In October 2007, Steffey filed a federal lawsuit that was settled out of court, with the sheriff's office paying a reported $475,000 to her. The color of truth is gray, and no one can deny that law enforcement officials have some of the toughest jobs around. But video can be a very compelling component in cases like this. When Tom Meyer called the sheriff to ask whether the settlement was an admission of guilt, he was told, "No reaction, Tom" and the sheriff hung up.

We mentioned Geraldo Rivera as one of the pioneers in TV investigative reporting. He had done some reporting about a corrupt judge in the Akron area and was aware of Cleveland's investigative reporters, especially Carl Monday. Geraldo had a syndicated show called *Now It Can Be Told*, and he made it a point to include Carl when he taped a series of segments in Cleveland in 1992. To get that kind of reputation, Carl had had to cover some serious and often dangerous ground.

Carl's investigative TV career started at Channel 8. He had done long-form investigative radio pieces on WERE when that station had been all news, but Carl knew pictures could tell the story even better. On television, it wasn't long before Carl's reports were getting a lot of positive attention for some less-than-positive topics. Here are some of the best.

Cleveland City Council president George Forbes held a lot of power. Some say he had more than anyone else in the city, including the mayor. You wanted something done? You'd better get the Forbes' seal of approval. One day Carl Monday got a tip saying Forbes and some other city officials weren't paying their water bills.

Now, Carl gets a lot of tips. On the phone, by mail, on the street . . . everyone thinks they have a huge story. Sometimes it's just a way to get back at an old boss or cause trouble for someone they don't like. Sometimes it's too good to be true.

The tip about Forbes and the water bills didn't seem like much. Even if it were true, anyone could dispute a bill or ask for an extension during a hearing with the Utilities Department. Yet all it took was a little investigation to find that Forbes hadn't squared up on his bill in more than a year, had never had a hearing, and still had water whenever he turned on his faucet.

Get a camera. Let's see how George explains this!

Here's the way Carl remembers it: "When I approached Forbes first thing on a Monday morning in February 1984, he was in no mood to talk about it. At first he shrugged it off with a smile, saying, 'It's no big deal. I don't have the money.' I came back with, 'You're the president of city council and you don't have the money to pay a $400 water bill?' Forbes started to get a little irritated. 'I don't have the money, OK?'"

Now, here the thing to consider. Forbes had known Carl for some time, back from their radio days. Forbes had had a show on WERE for a time, and Carl was already one of the best-known

COMING UP   8 NEWS

WHO DIDN'T PAY HIS WATER BILL? Carl Monday's face-off
against Cleveland City Council President George Forbes over an
unpaid bill became a classic moment in local TV news history.

reporters at City Hall. Why call attention to an embarrassing situation? And there was a camera, too. What happened next is considered by many to be the most classic Cleveland TV confrontation of all time.

For the next three and a half-plus minutes, Forbes tore into Carl. Carl recalls Forbes yelling, "You know, one of these days, I'm gonna take that F---ING camera and wrap it around your goddamned head. I ain't bullshitting you. Now take that goddamned camera out of my face!" Okay, it was getting serious, and the other council members saw it. As Forbes moved toward the committee room, he kept up the rant, and Councilman Lonnie Burten and some others tried to get him away from Carl. Forbes walked away, but it still wasn't over. He came charging back, turning the air blue, and yes . . . the tape was still rolling.

Rick DeChant was at Channel 8 at the time, and everyone knew this was the footage that folks would be talking about the next day. Station management decided to let Mayor George Voinovich get a look at it before it ran. The mayor stopped by the station, saw it in a production bay, shook his head, and said, "Run it!"

Oh, they ran it all right! Carl recalls, "I don't think Forbes ever expected us to air the outburst. But we did, thanks to some judicious editing. Remember, this was before social media. But it didn't stop viewers from bombarding the TV-8 switchboard with calls for Forbes' political scalp."

That story might have played a critical role in Forbes' political future—and the future of the city. Carl tells us, "A well-known city hall reporter told me years later that Forbes told him the incident might have cost him the mayor's race when he ran five years later. By the way, Forbes lost to then-city councilman Mike White, who we also reported had a $1,700 delinquent water bill."

Forbes had also had some well-documented confrontations with other council members. However, when he butted heads with Carl Monday, the event was preserved on video.

Oddly enough, as years went by, Forbes talked with Carl about the incident, claiming that he should have won the Emmy that year instead of Carl. At least he had a sense of humor and, truth be told, he didn't give Carl much room to talk anyway.

It's fair to ask: Why would you put yourself in that position? Why didn't Forbes square up with the city? Carl eventually found out. "Years later, as part of a 20th anniversary series on Fox 8, I updated the story," he said. "I went up to Forbes' office with cameras rolling . . . and handed him the Emmy I had won. Forbes gave a boisterous laugh—and the real story of why he hadn't paid his $400 water bill. He said he had used the money to buy his wife Mary a fur coat!"

Not all the stories have that kind of ending. Frankly, after stories like this next one, Carl's probably lucky to be alive.

The intersection of East 131st Street and Miles Avenue is on the city's southeast side, just down the road from Calvary Cemetery. In 1969 there was still some hope to bring the neighborhood back from impending blight, although white flight to the suburbs had been in full swing for some time and few businesses were investing in that neighborhood. A Giant Tiger store had closed, and a new Gaylord's department store had taken its place a few hundred feet down the road. But it wasn't drawing the kind of traffic it needed, and that store shut down, too. Part of it was converted into a night spot, the Len Roc Lounge. This was not a good place.

Carl recalls that the building was about the size of a small skating rink but was always filled beyond capacity. "The joint was a Garden of Eden, smack in the middle of the city. But it wouldn't be the first to feature open sex, prostitution, and drug activity.

"What separated the 'Roc' from the others is that we were told the place was 'protected.' In other words, whenever the cops tried to raid it, someone at the Roc got a phone call in advance. This turned out to be more fact than fiction, since the former commander of the Fourth District confirmed it for us in an interview."

Carl was working with an insider who was able to plant cameras in the ceiling. With real estate, it's location; with investigative reporting, timing is the key. Unfortunately, in this case Carl's timing was bad: a heating and air conditioning guy working on the building found the cameras and took them out before Carl got a chance to use them. Time for Plan B.

"We had a hidden camera planted in the false bottom of a purse brought in by an undercover female companion," Carl said. "Security patted everyone down and checked purses but never caught it the several times we took it in. The female would then go to the stall in the ladies room and hook the camera up and turn it on. Risky but it worked!

"Over a nine-month period in 1998, we documented all the sleaze and other illegal activity inside. We captured video of sex on tabletops and back rooms, and much more."

At the outset, Carl didn't know exactly what he was getting into.

"The day our first of many stories aired, we got two calls into the newsroom. Both were from area police departments saying that word on the street was, there was a contract on my life. When Fox corporate got wind of it, they called the FBI, and full-time security was assigned to me for the next several weeks."

Although station management never made it public, they thought they knew who was behind the threats, and the person in question didn't play around. It was a dangerous individual who wasn't afraid to get violent in public, including an incident in which he had put a loaded handgun into the mouth of a dance club employee and threatened to pull the trigger. Eventually the threats to Carl stopped and things cooled down, but for a while there was plenty of looking over the shoulder.

There have also been plenty of stories that got away. Here's one that Carl remembers well.

"Back in the mid-1990s I got repeated calls from a woman who said her daughter had been lured into the world of prostitution and drugs, and she pleaded for me to stop by her house to talk about it. By the third time she called, I asked her if I could record our conversation, and she approved. When I asked her who her daughter was hanging with, she told me the person's name. In fact, she told me he was sitting on their living room couch at that very moment.

Who? Nah. That's a big name. This woman may be a nut case. No way. He's too big to put himself in a position like that.

Even so, a few months later, Carl dug out the old tip and thought he'd check it out. He called the mom and got a disconnected number. Carl paid a visit to the house on the east side, knocked, and got no answer. A neighbor told him the woman had just passed away. The story hadn't seemed likely anyway, so it was time to move on. But as it turns out, that wasn't the end of the story.

A couple of years later, there was a huge drug bust on the city's east side. Among the suspects apprehended was the dead woman's daughter and Kevin Mackey. Yes, that Kevin Mackey! The very successful and popular head coach of the Cleveland State Vikings Kevin Mackey!

As Carl now remembers it, "We could have put a stop to the coach's lurid secret life long before. The mom had offered to let us put hidden cameras in her living room to document Mackey's destructive behavior that she says destroyed her daughter's life. Mackey's arrest ended his college coaching career. The story made international headlines. It was there for the taking, and I missed it. It reminds me to this day to take every tip seriously, no matter how outrageous it might sound."

"In my life, laundry and glamour don't mix!"

Dorothy Fuldheim Was Tough to the End

There are people in TV today who weren't even born when Dorothy Fuldheim left us on November 13, 1989, but they still owe "Big Red" a sincere debt of gratitude.

Dorothy was a pioneer in the truest sense of the word. She was the first woman to address the Cleveland City Club, and as ABC's Barbara Walters told the Associated Press after Fuldheim's passing, "She was probably the first woman to be taken seriously doing the news. She showed that age need not be a factor when you have the expertise and the energy. I knew Dorothy Fuldheim, and she made us all proud." Dorothy was brilliant and confident, but also eccentric and, at times, cantankerous.

Contrary to appearances, Dorothy Fuldheim did not have a life-time contract with WEWS. Granted, they would have been crazy to have let her go, but every few years, at contract renewal time, they talked turkey. Dorothy was never worried. In 1978, when her contract was up, she told the *Cleveland Press*, "The station has exercised its option. They had the right to choose if they want me or not. The option demands them to demand my services for another year, providing the remuneration is satisfactory. I'm sure it will be negotiated satisfactorily." Who wasn't sure?

Terry Moir once asked her, "Dorothy, you must have had a lot of opportunities to go someplace else. I don't understand why you never did." Dorothy replied, "I will tell you exactly why. Back in 1970 there was a shooting at Kent State, and I went on the air and said, 'They're murderers! Murderers!' When we got off the air, we got 10,000 phone calls and pieces of mail and I knew that I probably should have kept my mouth shut. I couldn't, because as far as I was concerned, that was murder." She said two or three days later, when the station was all abuzz about all these letters and calls demanding that she be fired, Don Perris came to see her. "I said to him, 'I would totally understand what you have to do.'" She said he came over, put his arm around her and said, "Dorothy, go home. I think you're ten feet tall." As Dorothy put it, "He showed me such loyalty. Do you think I would walk out on a guy like that? He told me to go home and get a good night's sleep. From that day on I knew I would never work anywhere else." And, of course, she never did.

Dorothy Fuldheim had a résumé that demanded respect even before the first TV broadcast in Cleveland, and she added to it on a daily basis. You were well advised to recognize that, too. There were stories about how she would fire people who angered her like the Queen of Hearts in *Alice's Adventures in Wonderland*—"Off with their heads!"—although most would agree that she was just letting you know that she demanded a certain level of performance. You might or might not have stayed fired. You could also get on her good side with chocolate (but not in a paper wrapper).

When the camera was on Dorothy, you just stepped back and let her say her piece. News anchor Ted Henry made the mistake of ignoring that fact in July 1984. When he interrupted her at the end of her commentary on the six o'clock newscast, Dorothy ripped into him for being rude. Henry apologized, but Dorothy shot back a glare and said, "You haven't soothed my ruffled feathers!"

Dorothy Fuldheim did well for herself and was smart with her money. She earned big paper for a long time, and took care of her family and friends. She also took care of herself. Even so, she was affected by the economy, although not in the same way it hit the average guy on the street. One day in 1977, she complained that the amount she paid her chauffer and maid made it difficult to put away $25,000 that year.

Her appearances off the air were just as spectacular as her TV work. Fuldheim drew attention just by showing up, and everyone wanted to reach out to her. She might have been just an inch over five feet tall, but that fiery red hair—every hair in place—and that Fuldheim aura made her bigger than life. Speaking engagements, book signings, awards dinners . . . you name it. It didn't matter who was being honored, if Dorothy was in attendance, she was the main attraction. That could also cause some very tense moments.

David Spero tells the story about his bar mitzvah party. His dad, Herman Spero, produced *Upbeat* and *Polka Varieties* and had clients at all the TV stations. Herman had a pretty gentle demeanor, but he could show another side when necessary.

David had invited a lot of his friends to the party, but it's who Herman had invited that drew concern: two of the biggest names ever in Cleveland TV. Both Dorothy Fuldheim and Ernie Anderson had RSVP'd and would be stopping by. Ernie Anderson's "Ghoulardi" show on WJW was at that time about as popular as a TV show could get, and he regularly poked fun at Dorothy Fuldheim on-air, yelling, "Doooorothy!" So, you have a bunch of twelve- and thirteen-year-old kids who want to get Ghoulardi's attention, and Dorothy Fuldheim is there at the same time . . . no, this isn't going to work.

David recalls his dad gathering him and his friends together before the big party, and the other side of Herman Spero appeared. In no uncertain terms, he told them, "You will NOT speak to or about Miss Fuldheim unless she addresses you first! And it's Miss Fuldheim! Got it?" The sound of hearts pounding in the chests of a bunch of bug-eyed boys sounded like a marching band, but it worked. They just looked at Ernie Anderson and "Miss Fuldheim," sitting together and laughing, from a distance. No one even dared whisper the name "Dorothy."

Dorothy was a strong personality, but that didn't mean she had free rein. When confronted she always held her own, yet some people didn't back down from the challenge. Tom Bush had been a stockbroker, a local TV executive at WKBF, and a voice-over artist and radio personality, and he pretty much knew all the media folks in town. Well known for his impressions, he had appeared in skits on *Hoolihan and Big Chuck* and later on *Big Chuck and Lil' John*. Bush was also a well-seasoned improvisational actor and was always in demand to emcee various events. People loved his act. Okay, not everyone. His impression of Cleveland Indians great Bob Feller and his frugality was so dead-on accurate and fall-down funny that Feller refused to appear anywhere Bush was on the bill.

Bush was the emcee for a 1983 dinner honoring Middleburg Heights mayor Gary Starr after his re-election. Dorothy had been asked to be the featured speaker. It had been a big year for Dorothy as well—her ninetieth—and she had made nationwide headlines by signing a three-year contract with WEWS.

Dozens of well-known politicians and media folks were in attendance, and Tom got in a good-natured dig at each of them. Big laughs, and then it was time for the main event. Tom had always had great respect for Fuldheim. He recalls, "I introduced Dorothy and asked her if she was doing anything different since she had turned ninety. She said, 'Yes. I've cut back racquetball to just twice a week.'" Everyone roared with laughter. Bush wasn't about to try to top that, so he sat down next to the podium.

Dorothy, however, apparently hadn't thought much of Tom's act and began railing about a sense of decorum and how disrespectful Tom had been to the guests. In fact, it became the focus of her speech! After a couple of minutes of this, Tom covered the side of his face with his hand and started imitating Chevy Chase's "blah, blah" routine from *Saturday Night Live*. Eyes half closed, head bobbing, tongue darting in and out of his mouth. The crowd started applauding and cheering, and Dorothy thought she had the audience in the palm of her hand. In reality, Tom had his face in his.

At many of her public appearances, Dorothy would take questions from the audience, and she answered them with the same attitude she brought to the TV screen. At one speech, she was asked what compelled her to take the direction she had in life when so many women of her generation were content to be homemakers. Dorothy straightened up and said without hesitation, "Sir, in my life, laundry and glamour don't mix!"

When Dorothy was on the air, she owned the screen. It was her show, and if you didn't like it, you could turn the channel or, if you were a guest, there's the door. You were there on her terms. It was also well known that she couldn't read all the books and press material that came to her office. As Dorothy put it, she wanted to approach the guests "fresh." And, because she was truly a legend, a lot of well-known folks wanted to meet her on and off the set. One of those was Gypsy Rose Lee, who had risen to fame as a stripper, but was also an author, actress, and lecturer.

Gypsy was co-hosting *The Mike Douglas Show* at KYW, and wanted to meet Dorothy. They booked her for a segment at Channel 5, and Dorothy opened with: "Now, tell me, dear. What is it you do for a living?" Needless to say, that didn't sit too well with Gypsy, who shot back, "Well, I'll tell if you tell me what you do!" There were a few anxious moments, but eventually they got on very well and even went out to lunch.

The bottom line was that no one told Dorothy what to say or do on TV. She had the first and final say, and her commentaries could depend on her mood that day. Mark Rosenberger was an executive producer at WEWS and worked closely with Dorothy. Every day he would stop by her office to offer suggestions from the news department about stories that were breaking or issues that she might comment on. He recalls that Dorothy would listen to recommendations and maybe shrug at what she heard. Later, she would go on the air and share her observations about tree bark or some other odd topic. Rosenberger's next regular visit was to the news director's office, where he would be asked, "What happened there?" They both knew. You didn't second guess Dorothy Fuldheim.

*   *   *

HOLDING COURT: Dorothy Fuldheim jetted around the globe covering stories from Prince Charles and Lady Di's wedding to the funeral of Anwar Sadat. When she was taken to a secret location in Northern Ireland for an interview with Bernardine Dohrn, she demanded to know why Dohrn kept her waiting. Here she is on the Concorde in 1981. *Eric Braun*

When Dorothy fell ill in her final years, her illness generated headlines and concern from across the country. It was Friday, July 27, 1984. She had struggled through a satellite interview with President Ronald Reagan, and right afterward, said she had a serious headache. People nearby knew it was more than that. Dr. James Kaufman, her personal physician and a close friend, was called to the station. He told *The Plain Dealer*, "When I got there, she was able to talk, but she was very lethargic." There was weakness on the left side of her body, but the pain was on the right side of her head. An ambulance rushed Dorothy to Mt. Sinai Hospital, where a brain scan showed a hemorrhage . . . and a blood clot the size of a fist! Because of the size of the lesion and the pressure it put on her brain, she was on the brink of death. They had to operate immediately.

Just before midnight she was wheeled into the operating room. Dorothy kept her sense of humor throughout the ordeal. She was as alert as could be expected, and when a member of the surgical team asked whether she had any allergies, she said, "Yes. To men!" After a couple of hours, the surgery was done and Dorothy was in critical but stable condition. There were several seizures afterward, but they were controlled with medication. Dorothy wasn't in pain, but she still in a very dangerous situation.

Mount Sinai wasn't prepared for the response when word got out that Dorothy was there. Their switchboard was jammed with calls from people asking about her condition. Even the White House tried to get through. The hospital couldn't handle the wave of calls. It finally had to have a special taped update on her condition. WEWS aired regular updates as well.

What people didn't know, at least at first, was that Dorothy had suffered a second stroke. This one affected her more, causing weakness on the right side of her body, slurred speech, and confusion. Her memory took a serious hit, and she couldn't remember the names of people who stopped by from one day to the next.

News of the latest stroke was actually held back for a few weeks because her doctors wanted to protect her privacy. Eventually, *The Plain Dealer* gossip columnist Mary Strassmeyer paid Dorothy a visit. She introduced herself, and Dorothy said, "Hello Mary." Strassmeyer asked whether she could interview her, and Dorothy agreed. She leaned against the side of a chair, holding the side of the face, and answering by moving her head to indicate "yes" or "no."

"Do you watch television?" Yes. "Do you like the food here?" Yes, but no more chocolates. She also didn't read *The Plain Dealer*. "Do you wish to go home to your condominium?" No. "Do you wish to stay here at the nursing home?" Dorothy nodded. Interesting, when you consider what would happen in the coming months.

When Strassmeyer prepared to leave, Dorothy told her, "I appreciate your coming. It is nice to see somebody alive once in a while."

Dorothy's doctor, James Kaufman, emphasized that Dorothy required close monitoring by a skilled nursing staff. Sam Miller, the Forest City Enterprises executive, who had been a close friend of Dorothy's for many years, stepped forward to make sure she received the best care possible. He told Strassmeyer, "I am under orders from Dorothy's three doctors to keep her in a nursing home. That's how it should be."

Dorothy was moved to the Margaret Wagner House of the Benjamin Rose Institute in Cleveland Heights in September 1984. She got excellent care, but it wasn't home, and she knew it. By January 1985, Dorothy wanted to return to her apartment, but everyone knew her health would not allow it. This is where the story took an ugly turn.

In a feature story in *The Lake County News-Herald*, Dorothy said she was being held against her will. She was unhappy and wanted to return to her apartment in Shaker Heights. Now, let's review: How many people her age want to be a nursing care facility, and how many realize the amount of care they really need?

A lot of people cared for Dorothy, but her special guardian angel was Sam Miller. The newspaper report quoted Dorothy as saying Miller was keeping her in the home, and that didn't sit well with him. He had a long-standing reputation for being tough, but fair. Miller told *The Plain Dealer* that the doctors knew best and he was following their advice. He said doctors told him, "Dorothy's circuits are down and some will never be connected again." The paper reported that Dorothy had other issues and would "confabulate . . . filling in gaps in the memory with detailed, but more or less unconscious accounts of fictional events." Miller went on to say, "I've known of this condition for some time, and I have tried to keep her 'friends' from dancing on her grave." He was backed up by three of Cleveland's most prominent physicians. Clearly, Dorothy Fuldheim was in the best hands possible.

Her condition touched a wide range of people. Dorothy was one of the most familiar Clevelanders, someone we had grown up watching on television, and now she was facing the final challenge. Phone calls poured in to WEWS and newspapers, asking about her. Most callers said they felt they knew her.

Friends from Channel 5 who visited her refused to discuss how she was doing. As one put it, "Sometimes being a good human being supersedes being a good reporter."

Milt Widder, a long-time columnist at the *Cleveland Press*, had known Dorothy for more than 40 years, and was also a resident at the Margaret Wagner House. He even made a point to sit with her at meals. Widder told *The Plain Dealer*, "She wants to get the hell out, but she's not ready to go. She doesn't have the mental capacity. Sometimes she's very good. Other times, she doesn't remember." *The Plain Dealer* even got calls from viewers who volunteered to care for Dorothy if she ever went home. The Margaret Wagner House staff was told not to let anyone see Dorothy, even if they were on the regular visitation list.

Some of Dorothy's friends backed her request to return home but again, Miller said that was not what she needed. "It is shameful at this time that this type of abuse is coming from her 'friends' who have no medical knowledge of her condition," he said. "I have given Dorothy's doctors permission to speak to these people, and they have done so. But apparently, the doctors don't tell them what they want to hear."

Miller continued, telling *The Plain Dealer* reporter, "I, in turn, can in no way benefit financially, psychologically or in any other manner while Dorothy is being kept in the Margaret Wagner House. I have no motives except one: I want Dorothy to get well. My wife, Maria, and I would be more than happy to have Dorothy in our home again. We lived together 85 percent of the time for three years before she suffered the stroke."

He went on to say, "I could hire nurses around the clock for Dorothy, but the life support systems are in the Margaret Wagner

House. We just do not have the facilities needed in case a woman of her age would need such a system."

Miller was backed up by Dr. Michael Devereaux, the chief of neurology at Mt. Sinai Hospital. He said Dorothy knew her name, but was "intellectually impaired" and had difficulty remembering where she was and even the time of year. He agreed she belonged at the Margaret Wagner House, and not just for the care. Devereaux said it was an environment that could "help protect her from people who have their own interests and motivations."

Dr. Robert White from Metro General Hospital, who also attended to Pope John Paul II after the attempt on his life, agreed. White said, "My assessment of her condition at the present time is that I see her intellectual abilities, decision making, memory, as limited, and I believe that reflects residual brain damage. I see her in need of professional care and the support the excellent Margaret Wagner House gives her. It is where she should be medically. I do not see Dorothy as a prisoner."

Plenty of friends stopped by to visit with Dorothy, but all pretty much went away with the same impression. Sam Miller gathered a few of them for a visit. They included Mary Strassmeyer from *The Plain Dealer*, and Dr. Robert White. Bishop Anthony Pilla from the Cleveland Catholic Diocese also came by with his assistant, Father Mike Dimengo. As they walked in, Dorothy asked, "Who are all these people?" Bishop Pilla had known Dorothy for some time, but he reintroduced himself. "Are you the one who operated on me?" Pilla calmly said no, and Dr. White said doctors had performed the surgery.

Dorothy seemed to recognize Mary Strassmeyer, and told her she was able to go home and "take care of myself." There was a walker nearby and Strassmeyer asked how mobile Dorothy was. She shot back, "I'm not going to give you a demonstration now!" As far as feeding herself at home, Dorothy said, "I never cooked in my life and I don't intend to start now." She finally got tired of the questions and told the group, "If you don't stop interrogating me, you may be dismissed." For a second they saw that spark that had defined Dorothy Fuldheim.

PERPETUAL MOTION: At an age when many have been comfortably retired for years, Dorothy Fuldheim continued to push herself to new limits. Here, she meets with her assistant in 1980. *Cleveland press Collection, Cleveland State University Archives*

Dorothy Fuldheim finally left us on November 13, 1989. She'd returned to Mt. Sinai Hospital a little less than a month before. She was 96 years old. Sam Miller remembered her in *The Plain Dealer*: "She was a great lady. We loved her dearly, as did the entire community. She will be missed, but she will never be forgotten or replaced." So many who knew Dorothy also saluted Miller, and gave their heartfelt thanks for his dedication to his friend of 30 years.

The accolades kept pouring in. ABC's Barbara Walters gave a lengthy tribute to Associated Press saying, in part, "She had verve, courage, and personality. She showed that age need not be a factor when you have the expertise and the energy. I knew Dorothy Fuldheim, and she made us all proud."

George Anthony Moore remembered his old friend this way: "Of course she was a pioneer for women in television. But she did commentary when no male or female in the country did commentary. She had a capacity for interviewing people and command of the language that doesn't exist anymore. She interviewed some of the greatest people in the world."

Bill Gordon had worked with Dorothy on *The One O'Clock Club* for seven years until 1964, and he remembered her as the "consummate professional." He said, "She was the end of an era. The end of a dynasty."

Dorothy loved her work, and WEWS gave her plenty to do. At one point, her commentaries were seen three times a day. She also maintained a hectic schedule of public appearances. Few people realized she had a good reason to do so many speeches. Dorothy's daughter, Dorothy Jr., had died in 1980, survived by her daughter, Halla Urman, who was in her 40s at the time and severely handicapped since birth. Halla was in the care of a retired nun in West Virginia, and Dorothy funded her care for life. That's why she accepted so many speaking engagements right up until she was hospitalized.

There was a certain aura, a type of elegance, that surrounded Dorothy. Part of it came from the way she carried herself and her meticulous appearance. Even when she was at the Margaret Wagner House, the staff continued to polish her nails, dye her hair, and apply just the right amount of make-up when she greeted visitors.

At the time of her death, Dorothy had been on the air longer than anyone in the history of the medium, 37 years—and she had started at WEWS when she was 54!

Let's end this with a smile. Producer Terry Moir had impressed Dorothy with a piece she had edited about her 91st birthday. They got along pretty well, and one day as they were walking down a hallway Terry was grumbling about finding the right guy. Dorothy said she was preaching to the choir. Terry couldn't believe what she heard. She said, "Wait a minute. You're Dorothy Fuldheim! There are guys in their seventies who would line up to be with you." Dorothy stopped, turned to her, and said, "My dear, I prefer older men . . . and at my age, there aren't many left!"

Epilogue

THINK ABOUT YOUR GRANDPARENTS or, if you were lucky enough to know them, your great-grandparents. As you grew up, the way you really got to know them was from their stories about the times they lived in. And maybe from looking through their old photo albums, their scrapbooks, and their book and record collections. The photos gave you a look at the world through their eyes, but what about the books and records? They showed you what entertained and informed them. All these things gave you insight into what shaped their opinions, and maybe even what helped them relax and made them happy. For folks who were alive in the second half of the twentieth century, you can add television to that list.

Sadly, so little of the early days of TV were preserved. Local programs were almost always broadcast live, and what little footage of it that was saved (on cheap film stock) was preserved by accident. No one thought they were filming history, or should have been filming it.

For younger readers, we hope we've given you an idea of who the people were on TV that the older generation talked about. They influenced your relatives and, just maybe, that was passed along to you.

Television showed us that Northeast Ohio is part of a greater whole. Some folks never thought beyond the boundaries of their neighborhood. But when you saw the Three Stooges joking with Captain Penny, or Dorothy Fuldheim interviewing Bob Hope, or Barbra Streisand on the *Mike Douglas Show*, you realized the Greater Cleveland area was pretty special, and an important place to be. They were practically in your neighborhood, and plenty of times the stars would promote a public appearance that might be right down the street from where you lived.

For baby boomers who are now entering the retirement phase, you look at TV like a friend who's always been there. When you're talking to people of your same age, you refer to folks like Miss Barbara, Jungle Larry, John Fitzgerald, Howard Hoffman, and so many others as though they were your late relatives.

Even the syndicated stuff, the bobbling puppets on *Supercar*, the creepy human mouths that joined with the so-called animation in *Clutch Cargo*, and early black-and-white anime of *Astro Boy*, take you back to a different time.

And let's not forget Lord Athol Layton, the host of *Big Time Wrestling*. He called the action with his sophisticated Australian brogue. "Bobo Brazil is a cagy ring veteran and . . . hello! He's introduced the Coco Butt!" Wrestling fans today would be scratching their heads. "You actually watched that stuff?" We can proudly answer, "Yeah. And you missed out!"

Hope you enjoyed this return to our TV past. We sure did, and if you ever want to take another mental vacation, we have a feeling there are plenty more pages to turn.

Acknowledgements

WE WOULD LIKE TO offer special thanks to a number of people. Some who are with us: Chris Andrikanich, Cliff Baechle, Lynn Bycko, David Gray, Brad Funk, Eric Funk, Rick Funk, Bianca Kontra, Tom Kontra, Jane Lassar, Angelina Leas, Rob Lucas, Don Mertens, Jenny Misciagna, Cate Misciagna, Cole Misciagna, Cora Misciagna, Theresa Misciagna, Tony Misciagna, Dave Sharp, Carol Story, Jane Temple, and Terry Williams. And, sadly, some who are gone: Bob Andrus, Dolores "Butchie" Coletti, Bruno "Brownie," and Doris "Chickie" Czapor, Dorothy Kensicki, Andrew Kopkas, George and Eleanor Oleska, Jeff Olszewski, Dick Pigon, Victor and Gloria Pruchinski, Georgianne Prusha, Doris Springborn, Steve and Tillie Tomko.

We also tip our hats to Bill Barrow and everyone at Cleveland State University's Special Collections Department and the Cleveland Memory Project, as well as the staff at the Cleveland Public Library's Newspaper Archives, and the amazing writers who documented this important part of our history. This book would have been so much more difficult to complete without them.

Bibliography

Unattributed Articles

"An Interview with Marty 'Superhost" Sullivan.'" *Northeast Ohio Video Hunter.* 2014.

"Angley's TV station will join the crowd." *Plain Dealer.* July 10, 1985.

"Barnaby calling it quits after 41 years on local TV." *Plain Dealer.* January 31, 1990.

"Bibb to replace Hambrick at TV 3 as co-anchor of the 11 p.m. news." *Plain Dealer.* January 4, 1985.

"Car hits TV newsman, woman.; 2nd kills her." *Plain Dealer.* January 17, 1985.

"Ch. 8 dismisses as 'nonsense' Mottl's accusation of vendetta." *Cleveland Press.* August 13, 1981.

"Channel 8 suspends sports director Mueller." *Plain Dealer.* March 24, 1981.

"Channel 8 taken off the block." *Plain Dealer.* April 19, 1989.

"Channel 8 takes WJW call letters." *Plain Dealer.* September 11, 1985.

"Ciofani is fired by Channel 5." *Plain Dealer.* February 1, 1990.

"Cleveland's own grand dame of TV." *Plain Dealer.* December 21, 1986.

"Cops: Church worker admits killing priest." *The Edwardsville Intelligencer.* December 11, 2002.

"Dorothy Fuldheim, 91, hospitalized." *Plain Dealer.* July 28, 1984.

"Dorothy Fuldheim's attackers get 60 days." *Cleveland Press.* January 20, 1982.

"Dorothy Fuldheim heads to Ireland to write for the Press." *Cleveland Press.* April 23, 1981.

"Drama made for TV." *The Repository.* February 17, 1989.

"Fast-food meal not as speedy as park lot looters." *Plain Dealer.* March 6, 1982.

"Former WKYC reporter to head CBS stations." *Plain Dealer.* August 30, 1990.

"Forecaster finds muggy conditions in Cleveland." *Plain Dealer.* September 2, 1991.

"Fuldheim's condition is critical." *Plain Dealer.* July 30, 1984.

"'Ghoul's lawsuit against 'Son' no scare tactic." *Beacon Journal,* December 11, 1987.

"Joel Rose." *Plain Dealer.* August 5, 2000.

"Joel Rose kills himself." *Record-Courier.* August 5, 2000.

"Mueller on way out at Channel 3." *Plain Dealer.* June 1, 1986.

"Power outage knocks TV 3 off air briefly." *Plain Dealer.* March 30, 1990.

"Private Clem & Mr. Mayor." *Time.* May 3, 1968.

"Tim Byrd leaves his post at WGCL." *Plain Dealer.* January 21, 1979.

"Vietnam stress cited in death at TV station." *Plain Dealer.* March 3, 1984.

Bylined Articles

Barnett, David. "The News as Show Biz." *Star*. Volume 2, Issue 9. August 2 - 22, 1974.

Barrett, Bill. "Amanda takes a nose dive." *Cleveland Press*. February 8, 1981.

———. "Ch. 3 news immobilized." *Cleveland Press*. September 11, 1979.

———. "First Ch. 61 Preview films not worth dressing up for." *Cleveland Press*. February 10, 1981.

———. "Koontz returning to weather beat." *Cleveland Press*. February 20, 1981.

———. "Preview discounts bootleg decoders." *Cleveland Press*. June 8, 1981.

———. "Video news is bland but enlivened by Ms. Fuldheim's raving, scolding." *Cleveland Press*. February 20, 1980.

———. "Weekend offers ghetto mish mash of talk shows, polkas and religion." *Cleveland Press*. February 22, 1980.

Bartimole, Roldo. "'Morning Exchange' has become morning sell; no controversy format of personal problems." *point of view*. Vol. 7, No. 17. June 6, 1975.

Bates, Daniel. "TV executives 'took drugs, went on bikini cruises and gave oral sex to clients', claims sexual harassment lawsuit." *Daily Mail*. January 14, 2014.

Bean, Don. "WJKW standoff ends in suicide." *Plain Dealer*. March 2, 1984.

Benson, Melinda J. "Rose coverage stinks." *Free Times*. August 23-39, 2000.

Brazaitis, Thomas J. "A glimpse into the minds of TV viewers." *Plain Dealer*. May 27, 1984.

Breckenridge, Tom. John P. Coyne, Rosa Maria Santana. "Joel Rose commits suicide." *Plain Dealer*. August 5, 2000.

———. Rosa Maria Santana, John P. Coyne. "Troubling questions remain in wake of Joel Rose's suicide." *Plain Dealer*. August 5, 2000.

Dawidziak, Mark. "'Morning Exchange' ends run with loving tribute." *Plain Dealer*. September 11, 1999.

———. "Stunned by suicide, friends, colleagues recall Rose as warm, witty." *Plain Dealer*. August 5, 2000.

Dissell, Rachel. "Lawsuit against WOIO Channel 19 alleges sexually hostile work environment in advertising department." *Plain Dealer*. January 13, 2014.

Dolgan, Bob. "Anchors away." *Plain Dealer*. May 28, 1989.

———. "Boot back in Portland as TV sports anchor." *Plain Dealer*. October 7, 1987.

———. "Channel 5's Stevens is a man on his way up." *Plain Dealer*. June 17, 1990.

———. "Donovan most dapper of anchors." *Plain Dealer*. May 28, 1989.

———. "Drennan hosts new panel show." *Plain Dealer*. May 28, 1989.

———. "Outspoken Coleman toned down." *Plain Dealer*. May 28, 1989.

———. "Shanley enjoying his latest stint." *Plain Dealer*. May 28, 1989.

Evet, Jerry. "Feud between Jim Mueller, Ch. 8 erupts into libel lawsuit." *Cleveland Press*. March 24, 1981.

Ewinger, James. "Channel 8 recouped by naming Mihalik." *Plain Dealer*. October 12, 1981.

———. "Channel 3 will team Boot with Bibb at 11." *Plain Dealer*. January 5, 1985.

———. "Entertaining sportscaster gives the Boot to sports." *Plain Dealer*. January 16, 1985.

———. "Expansion of local TV news has a ho-hum beginning." *Plain Dealer.* July 19, 1982.

———. "Faceless 100 endorsed TV 8 anchor." *Plain Dealer.* October 3, 1981.

———. "If strike hits WJKW, look for new faces." *Plain Dealer.* January 30, 1982.

———. "Mueller may be one of many leaving Channel 8." *Plain Dealer.* March 26, 1981.

———. "Tana Carli appointed to replace Hambrick." *Plain Dealer.* October 1, 1981.

———. "Tana Carli has magic TV touch." *Plain Dealer.* April 11, 1982.

Feder, Robert. "Retiring." *Chicago Media Served Fresh.* February 12, 2014.

Feran, Tom. "2 of local TV's best sign off." *Plain Dealer.* April 2, 1990.

———. "Beloved children's host plans stage return." *Plain Dealer.* October 11, 1990.

———. "Channel 43 set to mount a change." *Plain Dealer.* December 23, 1990.

———. "Channel 3 change rumored for years." *Plain Dealer.* March 17, 1990.

———. "Channel 3's pending sale spawns many questions." *Plain Dealer.* March 20, 1990.

———. "Channel 3's upcoming effort, 'First Report', has changes in staff." February 22, 1990.

———. "Facts, not frills." *Plain Dealer.* August 7, 1988.

———. "Feagler to leave TV-3 anchor position." *Plain Dealer.* May 6, 1993.

———. "Forces merged to buy station." *Plain Dealer.* December 23, 1990.

Feran, Tom. "Gillett quiets rumors of sale for Channel 8." *Plain Dealer.* January 17, 1989.

———. "NBC sells 51% of Channel 3 to S. Carolina group." *Plain Dealer.* March 17, 1990.

———. "No problem with your sound, TV-8 just hushing up on sale." *Plain Dealer.* April 19, 1989.

———. "Opinions varied on Wilma's move." *Plain Dealer.* December 22, 1990.

———. "Sale of Channel 3 proceeding." *Plain Dealer.* July 6, 1990.

———. "TV-3 says sale is good news." *Plain Dealer.* December 28, 1990.

———. "TV-43 tests news at 6." *Plain Dealer.* July 17, 1993.

———. "Tip leads to Demjanjuk exclusive for TV-3 reporter Orlousky." *Plain Dealer.* October 9, 1993.

———. "WJW-TV on the block again." *Plain Dealer.* September 14, 1990.

———. "WKYC to stay put, boss says." *Plain Dealer.* December 19, 1990.

———. "Wilma Smith switches to TV8." *Plain Dealer.* December 21, 1993.

———. "Workers want to buy WJW." *Plain Dealer.* June 16, 1988.

Fountain, John W. "Cleveland seminarian is held in rectory killing and arson." *New York Times.* December 10, 2002.

———. "Suspect in killing of priest reported fire in calm voice." *New York Times.* December 11, 2002.

Freligh, Becky. "TV news revolution here?" *Plain Dealer.* March 18, 1987.

Frolik, Joe. "Goodby, teddy bear." *Plain Dealer.* November 27, 1983.

Fulwood III, Sam. "Paper not reason for Rose's death." *Plain Dealer.* August 5, 2000.

Gard, Connie Schultz. "Jill Beach - Striving for ratings and recognition in Cleveland's TV news wars." *Plain Dealer Magazine.* August 26, 1990.

Gleisser, Benjamin. "Always Miss Barbara." *Cleveland Magazine.* May 1990.

Hanson, Debbie. "Marty Sullivan. Superhost." *clevelandseniors.com.*

Hart, Raymond P. "The laugh game. Now it's time to get back to basics." *Plain Dealer.* January 21, 1979.

Hicks, Jonathon. "New TV station ready for action." *Plain Dealer.* December 13, 1983.

Hickey, William. "Bill Flynn shakes the screen." *Plain Dealer.* February 18, 1979.

———. "Channel 8 lights 30 candles." *Plain Dealer.* December 16, 1979.

———. "The folly of TV-3." *Plain Dealer.* May 1, 1980.

Hitchcock, Craig. "Weekday fever." *Cleveland Press.* February 1, 1979.

Jones, Scott. "Move Over Hugh Hefner." *FTV Live.* January 15, 2014.

Jones, Scott. "We Brought Cake." *FTV Live.* May 23, 2013.

Kennedy, Jan H. "It's Ghoul vs. Son of Ghoul in character copying case." *The Repository.* December 11, 1987

Kingsley, Barbara. "TV news viewers fickle, merciless." *Plain Dealer.* August 13, 1983.

Kisner, Kathleen. "Peephole Paul." *Cleveland Magazine.* September 1993.

Morton, David. "Burdens of guilt." *Free Times.* August 23-29, 2000.

———. "Loose lips." *Free Times.* August 16-20, 2000.

———. "Questionable ethics." *Free Times.* August 16-20, 2000.

Myers, Ken. "Staying on the street." *Plain Dealer Magazine.* January 27, 1985.

Peer, Richard M. "TV reporter under fire." *Plain Dealer.* May 5, 1990.

Peters, Harriet. "Amanda is ready to go." *Cleveland Press.* January 3, 1978.

———. "Anne Mulligan is fulfilled." *Cleveland Press.* March 28, 1978.

———. "Jim Mueller to do PR work for builder." *Cleveland Press.* March 25, 1981.

———. "Rough sailing in store for Dick Goddard?" *Cleveland Press.* February 22, 1981.

———. "Weatherman is H on Cleveland." *Cleveland Press.* February 1, 1979.

Reesing, Bert. "Staff and nonsense." *Cleveland News.* January 23, 1960.

Riccardi, Maria. "Anchors away." *Plain Dealer.* November 4, 1984.

———. "Channel 3's loss is New York City's gain." *Plain Dealer.* March 26, 1985.

———. "Channel 8 employees are open to drug tests." *Plain Dealer.* February 13, 1985.

———. "D'Ascenzo leaving Ch. 8; Letterman irks 'Today'." *Plain Dealer.* August 23, 1985.

———. "Dorothy Fuldheim receives some guests." *Plain Dealer.* 21, 1985.

———. "Fuldheim condition improved." *Plain Dealer.* October 10, 1985.

———. "Fuldheim wants release; guardian heeding doctors." *Plain Dealer.* January 18, 1985.

———. "New ABC series loud but lacking." *Plain Dealer.* January 22, 1985.

———. "Minarcin will leave as WEWS Channel 5 co-anchor." *Plain Dealer.* July 9, 1984.

———. "Morning talk-show race takes ugly turn." *Plain Dealer.* July 1, 1985.

———. "New Channel 55 is getting under some skin already." *Plain*

———. "Public is protective of Dorothy Fuldheim." *Plain Dealer.* January 19, 1985.

———. "Reagan and fans worldwide sending Fuldheim their best." *Plain Dealer.* July 31, 1984.

———. "Solly replacing Hambrick on expanded TV 3 news." *Plain Dealer*. February 28, 1985.

———. "The ratings game eludes hapless Channel 3." *Plain Dealer*. March 16, 1985.

———. "The Weather Report - Local forecast: dry and serious." *Plain Dealer*. January 6, 1985. March 16, 1985.

———. "Yuppie puppies at TV 3 bark back." *Plain Dealer*. April 7, 1985.

Ricciardi, Maria and Luttner, Steve. "Fuldheim in coma after brain surgery." *Plain Dealer*. July 29, 1984.

Sandstrom, Karen. "Come rain or come shine." *Plain Dealer*. March 21, 1993.

Sandy, Eric. "Lawsuit filed against WOIO alleges on-the-clock drug use, sexual favors for ad clients." *Scene*. January 13, 2014.

Santana, Rosa Maria; John P. Coyne. "Evidence, Rose DNA don't match." *Plain Dealer*. August 4, 2000.

Santana, Rosa Maria. "Ex-TV host under investigation in porn case." *Plain Dealer*. August 4, 2000.

Scott, Wendy. "Joel Rose: Unexplained suicide, unfinished probe." *Morning Journal*. March 11, 2001.

Segall, Grant. "Mary McCrone won Emmy awards for WJW Channel 8 and elsewhere." *Plain Dealer*. January 5, 2010.

Seifullah, Alan A.A. and Strassmeyer, Mary. "Dorothy Fuldheim, TV news legend, dies." *Plain Dealer*. November 14, 1989.

Snook, Debbi. "Decision to air suicide tape still affects WEWS director." *Plain Dealer*. February 27, 1987.

———. "Gentzler will be missed: she is the genuine article." *Plain Dealer*. November 24, 1987.

———. "The good news and bad news: A report on Cleveland TV." *Plain Dealer*. 26, 1987. April 26, 1987.

———. "WKYC news boss quits." *Plain Dealer*. April 23, 1987.

Strassmeyer, Mary. "Dorothy Fuldheim suffers second stroke, is weakened." *Plain Dealer*. June 9, 1985.

Strassmeyer, Mary. "People Page." *Plain Dealer*. July 31, 1984.

Stringfellow, Eric. "Prince takes video skills into another arena." *Plain Dealer*. October 5, 1988.

Wallack, Todd. "Right conclusion, wrong reason." *Free Times*. August 23-29, 2000.

Whate, Rick. "Channel 67's 'Son of Ghoul' sued by 'dad'." *Canton Repository*, December 11, 1987.

Wolper, Joanna & Wolper, Allan. "Papering over the Joel Rose case in Cleveland?" *Editor & Publisher*. December 18, 2000.

Wyler, Linda. "Canton TV 'Ghoul' is vindicated." *Beacon Journal*. April 29, 1989.

OTHER BOOKS OF INTEREST . . .

Cleveland TV Tales
Stories from the Golden Age of Local Television
Mike Olszewski, Janice Olszewski

Remember when TV was just three channels and the biggest celebrities in Cleveland were a movie host named Ghoulardi, an elf named Barnaby, and a newscaster named Dorothy Fuldheim? Revisit the early days in these lively stories about the pioneering entertainers who invented television programming before our very eyes. Filled with fun details.

Ghoulardi
Inside Cleveland TV's Wildest Ride
Tom Feran, R. D. Heldenfels

The behind-the-scenes story of the outrageous Ghoulardi show and its unusual creator, Ernie Anderson. The groundbreaking late-night TV horror host shocked and delighted Northeast Ohio in the mid-1960s on Friday nights with strange beatnik humor, bad movies, and innovative sight gags. Includes rare photos, interviews, transcripts, and trivia.

"Captures a hint of the mania that made Ghoulardi a Cleveland idol in a sleepy era before long hair, drugs, assassinations, war and protests." – Columbus Dispatch

Big Chuck!
My Favorite Stories from 47 Years on Cleveland TV
Chuck Schodowski, Tom Feran

A beloved Cleveland TV legend tells funny and surprising stories from a lifetime in television. "Big Chuck" collaborated with Ernie Anderson on the groundbreaking "Ghoulardi" show and continued to host a late-night show across four decades—the longest such run in TV history. Packed with behind-the-scenes details about TV and celebrities.

"A vivid picture of an honest man in the insane world of television. Highly recommended." – Midwest Book Review

Read samples at **www.grayco.com**

OTHER BOOKS OF INTEREST . . .

Six Inches of Partly Cloudy
Cleveland's Legendary TV Meteorologist Takes on Everything—and More

Dick Goddard

Legendary Cleveland TV personality and pioneering meteorologist Dick Goddard celebrates 50 years on television with this grab-bag of personal stories, witty cartoons, fun facts, and essays about weather, pets, Ohio history, the TV business, and much more. Includes favorite stories about Dick told by friends and colleagues. Dozens of photos.

The Buzzard
Inside the Glory Days of WMMS and Cleveland Rock Radio—A Memoir

John Gorman, Tom Feran

This rock and roll radio memoir goes behind the scenes at the nation's hottest station during FM's heyday, from 1973 to 1986. It was a wild and creative time. John Gorman and a small band of true believers remade rock radio while Cleveland staked its claim as the "Rock and Roll Capital." Filled with juicy insider details.

"Gorman describes in exclusive, behind-the-scenes detail the state of rock 'n' roll from the early '70s to the late '80s, when just about anything happened and everyone looked the other way . . . Essential reading for musicians, entertainment industry leaders, and music fans." – Mike Shea, CEO/Co-Founder, Alternative Press magazine

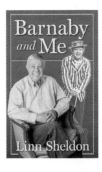

Barnaby and Me
Linn Sheldon

Pioneering children's TV host Linn Sheldon shares his own extraordinary life story. From a Dickensian childhood in Norwalk, Ohio, to Hollywood and back, Sheldon's odyssey includes celebrity, personal tragedy and self-destruction, recovery, and reflection. A remarkable mix of melancholy, hilarity, irony, and warmth.

"A revealing and hilarious look at [Sheldon's] career, which blossomed along with TV itself. The anecdotes are endless." – Sun Newspapers

Read samples at **www.grayco.com**